WORD PROCESSING WITH THE SINCLAIR QL

Mike O'Reilly

HUTCHINSON

London Melbourne Sydney Auckland Johannesburg

An HCP Product

Hutchinson & Co. (Publishers) Ltd
An imprint of the Hutchinson Publishing Group
17–21 Conway Street, London W1P 6JD

Hutchinson Publishing Group (Australia) Pty Ltd
PO Box 496, 16–21 Church Street, Hawthorne,
Melbourne, Victoria 3122

Hutchinson Group (NZ) Ltd
32–34 View Road, PO Box 40–086, Glenfield, Auckland 10

Hutchinson Group (SA) (Pty) Ltd
PO Box 337, Bergvlei 2012, South Africa

First published 1984
© Newtech Publishing Ltd

British Library Cataloguing in Publication Data

O'Reilly, Mike
    Word processing with the Sinclair QL —
    (The Hutchinson QL series)
    1. QUILL (Computer program)
    I. Title
    651.8   Z52.5.Q5

ISBN 0 09 158971 1

Set in Melior Medium
by FD Graphics Ltd, Fleet, Hampshire

Printed and bound in Great Britain by
Commercial Colour Press Ltd, London

CONTENTS

ILLUSTRATIONS

FOREWORD

by Nigel Searle
Managing Director, Sinclair Research Limited

It is difficult to imagine that Sinclair Research's first computer, the ZX80, was launched only four years ago. By today's standards it was extremely primitive. It had a memory of only 1 kbyte, BASIC that could handle only whole numbers, a flat keyboard, and the TV screen – black and white, of course – went blank whenever the computer had to do anything other than display its results. Each time a key was pressed, the screen flickered as the display was lost and then regenerated. The ZX80 cost £100 and launched a revolution.

Perhaps the most exciting aspect of the past four years is the way in which hundreds of businesses have come into existence to support – and profit from – the millions of Sinclair computers that have been sold. These businesses include publishers of magazines, books and software, as well as manufacturers of hardware add-ons. Most of them have been developed in a highly entrepreneurial way by people who were not previously businessmen, publishers or authors.

Sinclair computers are attractive to so many users because so much support exists for them. Those of us who work at Sinclair Research recognise that we will only attract such support as long as we continue to develop products worthy of it. We believe that, in the QL, we have developed a computer that will become the centre of a world-wide industry.

The ZX80 was a significant product because it enabled people to get their hands on a computer at a price that they could afford. The ZX80 did not compete in an existing marketplace; it created a new market of its own. Since the ZX80 was launched, many more powerful personal computers have become available at prices that could be afforded by some small businesses. Many individuals have looked at these new computers with envy. The computers they could afford no longer satisfied their need for computing power; the computers that could meet their needs were beyond their means. The QL is the answer to their problem. It provides very real computing power at a price well within the reach of many individuals.

Because the QL is so advanced, it is in many respects much easier to use than previous low-cost computers. But the range of its capabilities is enormous. It is not possible to anticipate all the potential applications for the QL. The features of SuperBASIC and of the four applications programs included with the machine – word processor, spreadsheet, graphics, and database manager – are described in the *QL User Guide*. But the hundreds of pages of this single volume cannot begin to anticipate the personal and business problems to which QL users will want to apply the computer's power.

I am pleased that Robin Bradbeer decided to edit this series of books about the QL. He has a knowledge of personal computers which is as deep as it is wide. He has a proven ability to explain to Sinclair users how to get the most from their machines. I am certain that these books will add enormously to the enjoyment and practical use that QL users will get from their computers.

INTRODUCTION TO THE QL SERIES

There can be little doubt that with the new Sinclair Quantum Leap computer, Sinclair Research Limited has a potential winner.

'Hands-on' experience with the QL and its associated software has convinced the authors and editors of this series of books that the QL is a computer to be taken seriously for a wide range of professional and business applications – in other words, to use a modern colloquialism – it's not just another computer 'hype'.

It would be wrong to say the QL is everything its makers claim for it. However, it is probably fair to say that the QL is almost everything it claims to be and, perhaps in the not too distant future when the bugs have been ironed out, its performance as a computer system might just surpass all expectations.

The Sinclair QL Series of books is intended to provide the user (or more accurately at the time of writing, potential user!) with clear and straightforward descriptions of the hardware and software and how they work. The books are as accurate as we can get them. Each author spent many man-hours with the QL, checking and cross-checking his work. In many cases this has involved a great deal of detective work – complete symmetry between the manual and the machine and its software has still to be achieved. Despite all our efforts, the reader may find some inaccuracies and misleading statements within the text. The QL is subject to continual revision and development and we can therefore only comment on the state of play at a precise moment in time – we cannot, as much as we would like to, forecast changes that Sinclair Research will make to later models of the QL.

That much said, the books are accurate as at June 1984, and their content reflects the latest manual available at that date and the QL with its ROM projecting from its rear.

All of us who have been involved with the production of this series of books have been greatly impressed by the QL and the Psion software packages. We hope that the quality of the books has mirrored as far as possible the quality of performance of the computer and its software.
Robin Bradbeer
June 1984

Acknowledgements

We would like to thank various people, without whose help we could not have produced these books; David Potter, Managing Director of Psion Limited and his colleagues who provided us with early working versions of the programs; Roger Morris of Sinclair Research, who in the face of constant badgering, never lost his cool and continued to send replacement cartridges whenever we broke the originals; Rex Malik for the use of his QL and his kitchen; Peter Rodwell and Alfred Rolington of *QL User Magazine* for the virtual theft of their QL and Carol at Newtech whose calm reassurance prevented authors from threatened suicide and self-disembowelment at the sight of a crashed Quill or unloadable Easel.

QL User is an EMAP publication

About the Author
Mike O'Reilly is a professional librarian working at the Polytechnic of North London, where he is also assistant manager of the community computing centre, demonstrating financial planning, word processing and database systems to the general public. Together with Robin Bradbeer he founded the North London Hobby Computer Club, which is the largest in Europe.

PREFACE

One of the UK's premiere computer magazines, *Which Office System*, recently conducted a reader survey. It showed that 78% of their readers were already using word processors. When the readers were asked to look ahead 5 years, 98% envisaged using a word processor. This result astonished the editors of the magazine. Did 2% of their readers really intend to introduce an office system without a word-processing facility? It was inconceivable!

Word processing in the home has not grown to the same extent as in the office. The programs for so-called home computers are so rudimentary that they hardly merit the term word processor. However this situation has now changed. Computer industry analysts have long been predicting the arrival of the computer equivalent of the Ford Model-T motor-car. Such a machine would provide for the general public the kind of computing power presently reserved for the business community. That machine has finally arrived – it is called the QL. The combination of the QL and Quill represents a word-processing facility that would not be out-of-place in any office in the land.

This book is about word processing on the QL. It is based upon my experience at the North London Community Computer Centre where we demonstrate a wide range of word processors to hundreds of customers a year. You will not need any technical background or any prior knowledge of computers to understand the topics covered in this book.

A word-processing system is comprised of two basic elements:

- Hardware – a computer, a VDU (screen) and a printer.
- Software – the word-processing program.

Keyboard
The book begins with a discussion of the QL's keyboard. Newcomers to computing are often intimidated by a computer keyboard that contains a large number of keys not normally found on conventional typewriters. The function of these special keys is explained with particular reference to their use in computer programs like Quill.

VDUs
Unlike some other computers, the QL does not come with an integral VDU. So what kind of screen should you use? Will any old television be suitable? Should you rush out and buy a colour monitor? What is the difference between a television and a monitor? The section on VDUs will answer these and other questions. It will also offer specific guidance on the factors you should consider before purchasing a monitor.

Printers
A word processor without a printer is about as useful as a typewriter without paper. There are so many printers on the market that selecting a printer to match your requirements can be a very difficult decision. The chapter on printers describes:

● the different kinds of printer
● how they work
● the advantages and disadvantages of each kind of printer
● the problems you should expect when using a printer

Word processing
Chapter 3 is your introduction to the wonderful world of word processors. If you have never used a word processor, you will be amazed at the facilities they offer: two-fingered typists can dispense with their correcting fluid; membership secretaries will see their work cut in half and authors can produce camera-ready copy for their publishers.

Quill
By this point in the text you should be ready to exploit the powerful features provided by Quill. The next three chapters describe all the Quill commands – what they are and how to use them. Quill is good but it is by no means perfect. Accordingly I have outlined various ways to overcome its limitations.

Spelling checkers and other writing aids
Did you know that in the near future QL owners will be able

to buy:

- Spelling programs that will check your text against an electronic dictionary?
- Thesaurus programs that will answer questions like 'What are the synonyms for *evil*?', 'What are the antonyms for *good*?'
- Indexing programs that will automatically generate an index of all the keywords in your documents?

Chapter 10 speculates about what features you might expect to find in these programs so that you can make a knowledgeable assessment of their strengths and weaknesses.

Presentation
The presentation of your documents is nearly as important as their content. Poor presentation may obscure the information you wish to convey and may even deter the casual reader from attempting to grasp what you are saying. Chapter 11 introduces you to some of the basic 'rules' of good layout. In particular it draws your attention to how a careful use of space leads to much more readable documents.

Communicating with other computers
Word processing is no longer exclusively concerned with producing printed documents. The trend is increasingly towards generating text for transmission to other computers. Chapter 12 explores Prestel, electronic mail and computer-to-computer communications. Guidance is given on purchasing modems and the necessary communications software.

Health risks of VDUs?
Many people are unaware of the controversy surrounding the health-hazards of using VDUs. Chapter 13 discusses this important topic with reference to the most authoritative document yet produced on the subject: The Health and Safety Executive's *Guidance Note on VDUs*.

Mike O'Reilly
June 1984

Chapter 1

BECOMING FAMILIAR WITH THE QL

If the QL is your first computer you are probably very excited. If previously you have owned one of the many 'home' computers on the market, then you are almost certainly more excited than the first-time buyer. This may seem paradoxical but it is likely to be true. Let me explain. A computer is not like the other electrical goods you own. These other household appliances are designed to meet a specific need. For example a washing machine washes clothes. A twin-tub and an automatic washing machine differ only in the ease and speed with which they wash clothes. Similarly hi-fi systems vary in the 'features' they offer but essentially they all perform the same function: to record and reproduce sound.

A powerful microcomputer like the QL is not designed for one specific application; the range of applications is only constrained by the imagination of the user. The experienced computer-user is more keenly aware of the breath-taking opportunities offered by the QL than the novice. If you are new to computing then you will need to understand some aspects of the design of the QL if you are to realize its great potential.

The keyboard

The QL has a conventional typewriter-style keyboard with 65 keys. The alphabetic keys conform to the traditional **QWERTY** layout – the first six keys on the top row of letters spell out the word QWERTY. In addition to the standard set of typewriter keys, you will notice a number of unfamiliar keys that are unique to computer keyboards:

Figure 1.1   The QL keyboard

CTRL
ALT
ESC
5 keys labelled F1 to F5 called **function keys**
4 arrowed keys called **cursor keys**.

Using these keys requires some understanding of how a keyboard works.

Each time you depress a key it generates an electrical signal which is converted internally into a **unique code**. Each character has a different code. There is an internationally agreed standard for these codes called the American Standard Code for Information Interchange (ASCII).

All the common characters are covered by this standard including the upper and lower case letters, the digits 0 to 9 and the punctuation marks. For example if you typed in **Aa1%** you would generate the following codes:

01000001   (ASCII A)
01100001   (ASCII a)
00110001   (ACIII 1)
00100100   (ASCII %)

I have used the **binary number system** to represent these codes because this is the system used internally by the computer. If you are not familiar with this system, relax; a knowledge of the binary number system only becomes really important if you delve deeply into the mysteries of machine-code programming.

SHIFT

When you press a key, a character appears on the screen. As with a typewriter, if you press the **SHIFT** key in conjunction with a letter key you will generate the capital letter. The uppermost symbols on the top row of the keyboard are also generated in conjunction with the SHIFT key. Now press the SHIFT key on its own. What do you see? Nothing happens. The SHIFT key is one of a number of keys on the keyboard which do not produce a printable character.

Space

Please note that a 'space' *is* a printable character and it too has its own unique ASCII code. A very annoying feature of the keyboard is that the space bar does not generate a 'space' if the SHIFT key is depressed.

Although the keyboard on the QL resembles a typewriter keyboard, it is in fact fundamentally different. Every time you press a key on the QL, you are giving the computer a **command** or **instruction**. Most of the time you are simply telling it to place a specific character on the screen. So if you hit the 'A' key, the computer 'obeys' your instruction and stores an 'a' in the QL's memory and this character is then displayed on the screen.

However, the QL is such a powerful computer that it will be used in literally thousands of different applications. Each program will have its own set of commands. For example **Quill** has over 40 different commands: delete a word, load a file, set tabs, set margins, etc. These commands should be easy to use and require as few keystrokes as possible. Short of having a keyboard the length of a piano's, it is simply not practical to have a **dedicated** key for each command.

The designers of the QL have solved this problem by providing a set of keys:

CTRL   known as the CONTROL key
ESC   known as the ESCAPE key
ALT   known as the ALT-MODE key
F1..F5   known as FUNCTION keys

which can be used in application programs to signify instructions to the computer. These keys are used either on their own or in conjunction with other keys on the keyboard to generate commands. For example when you are using Quill you may

● obtain help at any time by pressing **F1**

● print a document by pressing **F3** and **P**

Just which combination of keys are used to indicate commands will vary from program to program.

It is important to realize that it is precisely because these special keys *do not* produce a printable character that enables them to be used as commands. This is obvious if you think about it. Imagine you are typing in a document using Quill and you decide to stop for the day. You will need to give the appropriate instruction for exiting from the program. If you type in any of the normal printable characters, Quill will assume you are still typing in your text. However if you hit one of the special keys, Quill detects that it is not a text character and assumes you are giving it a command.

The cursor

The group of keys with arrows on are called the **cursor** keys. Their purpose is to tell the typist where he or she is typing on the screen. The cursor is displayed as a flashing coloured block of light. Pressing the arrow keys moves the cursor about the screen. Once you have positioned the cursor, anything you type will be displayed at that location. As you type, the cursor moves along to the right just like the carriage on a typewriter.

Delete

The QL does not have a delete key. On most keyboards there is a single key which will erase the character to the left of the cursor. To delete a character on the QL, you press the CTRL and ← keys simultaneously. This will be no great hardship since the keys are adjacent to each other.

Reset

On the right-hand side of the QL there is a little recessed button called the **reset** key. The reset button is not an on/off switch; the only way to switch off the QL completely is either to switch it off at the power point or remove the power lead from the socket at the back of the QL. Incidentally, if possible always switch off at the power point since repeated insertion and removal of the power lead can lead to a damaged socket. When you press the reset button, the machine acts as if you have just switched it on. The QL erases all the programs currently residing in its memory and the Sinclair logo reappears. Make sure you remove the cartridges from the Microdrives before resetting the QL otherwise they may be corrupted.

You may be asking why you need a reset key. Frequently – and unfortunately I mean frequently – the programs you are running 'hang-up'. Essentially this means that no matter what keys you hit, no matter what commands you give it, the machine just ignores you and carries on with what it is currently doing. In this circumstance you have no option but to press the reset key in order to re-establish communication with the machine. You may also reset the QL by hitting CTRL and SPACE. This combination of keys has been carefully chosen to ensure that you do not accidentally reset the machine. As you might expect, resetting the machine is normally an act of despair!

CAPS LOCK

Computer programmers generally use capital letters in their programs. It becomes very tiring and irritating to keep a finger continually on the SHIFT key while you type in long programs. On cheaper microcomputers you press the SHIFT key to obtain lower-case letters. This assists the computer programmer but is very confusing to everybody else. The QL has a more traditional solution to this problem. Once the CAPS LOCK key has been depressed all letters appear in upper case, while the other keys are not affected. However it is easy to fall into the trap of assuming that the CAPS LOCK key is the same as a shift lock key which you find on many typewriters. If you make this mistake you will discover, for example, that the number 5 appears when you really wanted the % sign.

ENTER

The largest key on the keyboard is the L-shaped **ENTER** key. Although this key resembles the carriage-return key on a typewriter, in fact it performs a complete function on the QL. As its name suggests, its primary purpose is to signify to the QL that a particular sequence of operations have been completed. For example, when you are typing in programs, each line of the program is terminated by pressing the ENTER key. The ENTER key indicates to the QL that you have completed that program statement and you want it incorporated into your program.

Keyboard hardware

The keys are of the two-shot moulded type which ensures that the characters will not wear off, no matter how much they are used or abused. Just like the writing in a stick of rock, the character goes all the way through the key. The keys are concave in shape, i.e. they are shaped like a very shallow cup. The touch typist will be disappointed to discover that the 'home' keys – F and J – are not physically distinguished from the other keys. On top-class keyboards these keys are slightly more concave than the rest of the keys. This enables the typist to sense that the fingers are correctly positioned on the keyboard.

On the other hand the QL does have adjustable feet that alter the angle of the keyboard. Research suggests that the most comfortable angle for the keyboard is about 12° to the horizontal. At this stage, with the hands at rest, the fingers should lie naturally on the 'home' row of keys.

The screen

'What screen ?' you may ask. Unlike many other computers, the QL does not have an integral Visual Display Unit (VDU), i.e. a screen. Therefore we need to address the problem of what are the advantages and disadvantages of the various types of VDUs that are compatible with the QL.

For our purposes VDUs may be divided into two categories: conventional televisions and video monitors. Corresponding to these two types of VDU, there are two 'output ports' on the back of the QL. The one labelled **UHF** is used in conjunction with a television, the other labelled **RGB** connects to a monitor.

Television pictures are broadcast on the UHF and VHF wavebands. These signals are referred to as **RF** signals. Technically it is not possible to send video signals (the pictures) directly through the atmosphere. Instead those clever television engineers code the video signals by modulating the RF signals. This may sound terribly complicated but bear with me. This process may be likened to putting parcels on a railway train.

Your aerial picks up the signals and then feeds them into your television. Then the television has two problems to solve: first it has to filter off the parcels (the pictures) from the train (the RF signal); secondly it has to distinguish the parcels belonging to the different television channels. A television receiver has a number of specialized circuits for tuning into the various channels and for extracting the picture information from the RF signal.

Monitors

A video monitor is essentially a television set without all this fancy electronics for decoding the RF signals. In fact it is possible to convert your domestic television into a monitor. If you do modify your television in this way, you would no longer be able to receive television pictures off the air (this is a job for an expert – it is very dangerous to touch the inside of a television).

The QL produces a pure video signal but in order to feed an ordinary television it has to convert the video signal into the form the television expects. It therefore has to generate the same sort of signal that normally comes to the television through the atmosphere. The process of modulating the RF signal and then having it demodulated inside the television set inevitably degrades the quality of pictures you receive. A far better approach is to feed the QL's pure video signal

Figure 1.2   The QL connected to a monitor

directly into the video circuits of a television. A VDU
capable of receiving a pure video signal will display far
sharper pictures than a television.

The difference in picture quality becomes very important
when we consider word processing. Because a monitor
receives a pure video signal, it is able to display
comfortably lines of up to 80 characters, whereas a
television will find it difficult to display even 64-character
lines. In particular, smaller characters are much easier to
read on a monitor while graphics (and games!) are
immeasurably improved by the sharper colours and lines.

The most inexpensive option for most people is to use
their domestic television. However you must realize that
watching TV and using a television as a VDU are
completely different experiences. Continual reading of
large amounts of text on a screen is visually very tiring if the
resolution of the characters is poor. My advice is that if you
intend to do a large amount of word processing then beg,
borrow or buy a good monitor. You will not regret it. A
compromise solution is to use one of the hybrid TV/
monitors now on the market. Generally they have the
advantage of being able to be used as a normal television.
Unfortunately these sets are relatively expensive at the
moment.

Colour

It is possible to create any of the colours of the rainbow by an appropriate mixture of the three primary colours: *red, green, blue*:

Colour	Mixture
Black	No colour
Red	
Green	
Blue	
Yellow	Red and green
Magenta	Red and blue
Cyan	Blue and green
White	All three colours

A colour television screen is a mosaic of red, green and blue dots. On a typical screen there will be upwards of one and a half million of these dots! A particular colour can be produced at any part of the screen by illuminating a suitable combination of the coloured dots. Inside the television there are three so-called **colour guns** corresponding to the three primary colours. Each gun only illuminates dots of a corresponding colour on the screen. The video signal controls the firing of the guns which in turn determines which colours are generated on the screen. Of course the viewer is unaware of this process because the individual dots are too tiny to be seen by the human eye.

RGB

If you look at the technical specifications for colour monitors, you will notice that two types of video input are mentioned: composite video and RGB. A composite video signal combines the three colour signals into one colour signal. The monitor receives the composite signal and then splits the signal back into the three separate colour signals which control the colour guns. As you might expect, there are several different methods for producing a composite video signal. In this country we use the **PAL** system for coding video signals. Other countries use totally different systems. For example, France uses a system known as **SECAM** while the **NTSC** system has been adopted by the United States.

The QL is able to produce not only a composite video output but also an RGB video output. With an RGB video signal the three colours are fed separately into the monitor. The monitor therefore does not have to split up the signal into three colour signals before feeding them to the colour guns. The RGB signal produces a sharper picture because it does not have to go through the mixing and splitting process of the composite signal.

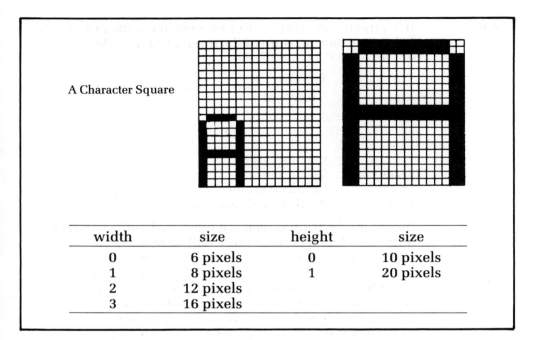

A Character Square

width	size	height	size
0	6 pixels	0	10 pixels
1	8 pixels	1	20 pixels
2	12 pixels		
3	16 pixels		

Figure 1.3   Standard character available on the QL

Pixels

To understand how text is displayed we require some understanding of how the QL 'sees' a screen. The picture displayed on your VDU by the QL may be considered as being composed of a large number of dots called picture elements (pixels). These are not symonymous with the coloured dots that cover the surface of the screen. The QL has two modes: in high-resolution mode it treats the screen as if it is a grid of 256 rows each containing 512 pixels; the low-resolution mode is a grid of 256 rows containing 256 pixels.

To display a single character, the computer uses a rectangular array of dots. This grid is called a **dot-matrix**. Figure 1.3 shows a typical example of characters generated on the QL. In general the more dots you use to define a character the sharper the image. In high-resolution mode on a monitor, the QL is capable of displaying lines of 85 characters. Each character is formed from a 6 by 10 dot-matrix. Obviously the width of the dot-matrix determines how many characters you can display on a line. To arrive at the figure of 85 characters you simply divide the number of pixels across the screen (512) by the width of the dot-matrix (6) – plus a couple of unused pixels. Surprisingly the QL uses the same 6 by 10 dot-matrix to display 64 characters across an ordinary television. Normally this would produce very indistinct text but the QL cleverly spaces out the characters to increase the legibility.

Bandwidth

If you look at advertisements for monitors you will observe that they all specify a maximum bandwidth for the signal they can receive. If you have a PhD in electronics you will understand what it means; if you have an O-Level in Serbo-Croat you accept your ignorance and hope for divine guidance (you certainly won't get any guidance in the shop!) It is said that in Ancient Greece they used to kill a messenger who brought bad news. I hope you don't resurrect this tradition because I bring the grave tidings that bandwidth is important and we need to understand it, at least in general terms.

For our purposes, bandwidth is a measure of picture sharpness. It is usually stated in so-many Megahertz (MHz), but unlike inflation, the bigger the number the better. A monitor with a bandwidth of 24 MHz will display far sharper pictures than a colour television with a bandwidth of about 4.5 MHz. The price of a monitor is directly related to its bandwidth.

If we wish to avoid unnecessary expenditure, we must estimate the bandwidth that will cope with the high-resolution graphics of the QL. In high-resolution mode, the QL displays 512 pixels to a line. To calculate the bandwidth requirement, we use the rule of thumb that 1 MHz is required to differentiate between every 60 pixels on a line. To get a good picture on the QL we need a monitor with a bandwidth of about 8 MHz (512/60), i.e. 8 MHz is required to display 512 pixels to a line. This, I hope, explains why a colour television with a bandwidth of about 4.5 MHz is unable to cope with lines of 80 characters.

Choosing a monitor

If you intend to buy a monitor you must first test it out on your QL. If the shop refuses to let you test the monitor with your QL, go elsewhere. There are a number of simple tests you can use to determine whether the monitor is going to be satisfactory or not:

1   Fill the screen with text. The QL will generate 25 lines of 85 characters. Check to see if the text is readable at your normal viewing distance. Vary the colour of the text and the background colour. In particular check the display of green and white characters on a black background. These are the colour combinations you will probably be using with Quill. Move into low-resolution mode and select two colours like yellow and green which are adjacent in the spectrum. See if you can easily read yellow text on a green background. This will really tax any monitor since this is the minimum contrast possible between two colours.

2   Type a screen-full of plus signs (+). They should be the same size and width everywhere on the screen. Pay special attention to the edges of the screen which is where distortion is most likely to appear.

3   Finally test the power supply with a totally white screen. There should be constant brightness across the screen. If the brightness begins to fade slightly then the power supply is not as good as it might be. Sometimes it is easier to detect this effect by filling the screen with black characters on a white background. If the contrast between the text and the background diminishes, you can be pretty sure that you have an inadequate power supply.

Now repeat this procedure with at least two other monitors. You will be amazed at how quickly this approach sharpens your critical faculties. When you begin the first monitor looks really great; at the finish you will be discriminating between colour hues, picture shimmers, character resolutions, etc.

It is vital that you select your monitor with some care; you will be spending literally thousands of hours in front of it. A few hours spent in choosing a monitor is a worthwhile investment of time.

Chapter 2

PRINTERS

If you are using the QL for word processing then eventually you will wish to transfer your precious prose on to paper. After all there is usually little point in viewing text on a screen or simply storing it away indefinitely on a Microdrive. You will need a printer. And then I am afraid your troubles really begin.

The variety of printers on the market is truly bewildering. Although a printer may exist that perfectly matches your needs and your pocket, it is more likely that your final choice will be a compromise between price and performance. Let us identify the factors that might influence your choice of printers:

- compatibility with the QL
- cost
- print quality
- special print features
- speed
- noise and vibration
- paper handling
- reliability

Compatibility with the QL   In order to connect a microcomputer to a printer it is necessary to have a device that matches the computer to the printer. This device is called a printer interface. A printer interface is an electronic circuit that converts the electrical signals from your computer into the type of electrical signals that your printer can understand. Printers usually come with either an **RS232C** interface or a **Centronics parallel interface**.

The QL's output port labelled **SER1** is an integral RS232C printer interface. Sinclair has promised that in due course a parallel interface will be made available as an optional extra. Until such time the only printers that are compatible with the QL are those which have an RS232C interface.

It would be nice if I could say that once you have found an RS232C compatible printer your headaches are over. Alas this is not the case. You still have to connect the QL to the printer with a suitable cable. In theory the RS232C is an internationally agreed standard for connecting peripherals (e.g. printers, modems, etc.) to computers. This standard also effectively defines how the cable should be connected. Yet the fact that both the QL and the printer claim to abide by the standard is no guarantee that you can connect the two together.

At one time the Centronics parallel printer interface was almost the *de facto* standard for the microcomputer industry. It is to be hoped that the promised Sinclair parallel interface is Centronics compatible, for, unlike the RS232C, you can be reasonably confident that two Centronics compatible machines will actually work together.

To ensure that the QL is going to work with a prospective printer, the best advice is to:

1   See a QL working with the printer before you buy it.

2   Make sure you either buy a **functioning** cable with your printer or your printer dealer gives you the *exact* specification for making up such a cable. If you leave the shop without either the cable or the information you are almost certain to face hours of frustration just trying to get your printer working.

Cost

The printer market is very competitive at the moment and prices are falling fast. Naturally you will wish to obtain the cheapest printer that meets your requirements. However, there are other considerations over and above the price/performance calculation. For example, if you are in the middle of printing some urgent work and your printer breaks down it may be necessary to borrow a friend's printer. In the light of the discussion on printer interfaces you should now realize that this may not be as easy as it sounds. If you decide to buy a *brand name* it is much more likely that you will know someone who has a similar printer.

Print quality   The most important factor in selecting a printer, apart from the cost, is the **print quality**. As you might expect there is a direct relationship between print quality and price. There are exceptions to this rule, but cheap printers that generate high-quality print suffer from other disadvantages: very slow, noisy, etc. The print quality you need depends upon the kind of documents you are going to create and who is going to read them. If the main use of your word processor is to produce documents and letters for customers then you are going to require a print quality comparable with a golf-ball typewriter.

Types of   **Daisywheel printers**
printer   Printers that produce text of this quality are called 'letter-quality' or 'correspondence-quality' printers. The only reasonably priced (under £800) printers capable of producing good-quality print are daisywheel printers. A daisywheel printer uses a light plastic wheel with between 96 and 128 spokes radiating from the hub. At the end of each spoke is a single embossed character (a **fully formed** character) like those on a typewriter. To print a character the wheel is rotated at high speed until the character is aligned with a print hammer. The hammer strikes the character onto a ribbon and this in turn onto the paper. This mechanism ensures accurate positioning and uniform striking, resulting in superb print quality. If you want a variety of typefaces you simply swap the daisywheel for another with a different character set.

Dot-matrix printers
The most popular alternative to the daisywheel printer is the dot-matrix printer. The print quality of dot-matrix printers is synonymous in the public mind with computer output. If you are only bashing out internal memos, occasional letters to friends or the minutes of your social club then a dot-matrix printer is just what you need.
    The characters produced by a matrix printer are formed from a dot-matrix in the same way that the QL creates characters on the screen. The printhead is a metal block containing a column of 'needles'. Each of these tiny metal rods can be selected independently and forced onto the ribbon. To generate a particular character, the printer selects the appropriate combination of rods. These rods are 'fired' out of the printhead and, on striking the ribbon, they create the impression of a character on the paper. Because you can actually see the dots that compose the characters, the overall impression is far short of that produced by even a manual office typewriter. However matrix printers are improving all the time.

The latest generation of matrix printers claim to produce 'near-letter-quality' (**NLP**) type. This improvement in type quality is achieved by reducing the space around the dots; it is this space which tends to dilute the visual impact of the letters. One method involves printing a line of text then the printer rolls the paper up the width of one dot and reprints the line. On the second pass over the line, the characters are offset by one dot compared to those produced on the first pass. This effectively eliminates the 'dotty' appearance of the text since the characters now appear to be formed from solid lines rather than dots. This facility is termed **double-strike** printing. A related but alternative method of creating 'solid' style type is to use **emphasized** or **bold** printing. It is very similar to double-strike mode except that on the second pass the character is printed one dot to the side of the first line. Both methods considerably improve legibility, but the label 'near-letter-quality' is a a pretty accurate description.

One of the most important elements in print quality is the presence or absence of true **descenders**. This term refers to the bottom half of the lower case letters: 'g', 'j', 'p', 'q' and 'y'. The **tails** of these letters should descend below the base-line of the text. A document produced without true descenders is appreciably more difficult to read than one with descenders.

Matrix printers find it difficult to reproduce clearly certain characters. Look especially at the following symbols: M, 4, 8, @, $ and &. This is particularly important if you are likely to be using high-quality paper. Some brands of superior paper have an embossed texture and this may seriously affect the legibility of these characters. It is only sensible to test a printer with the range of papers you commonly use.

Special print features

I have already mentioned that with a daisywheel printer you have the capability of using different typefaces by simply slotting in a fresh daisywheel. In practice you are unlikely to want the hassle of swopping print wheels in the middle of printing a document. Theoretically matrix printers can change typeface under software control. So you can alter the text to bold, italic, double-strike, etc., without having to stop the printer. Most matrix printers come with one or two built-in character sets.

The latest matrix printers are so versatile that in principle it is possible to create your own specialized character sets. For example, an Arabic character set might be used if you have customers in the Middle East. Technical writers will delight in being able to define some of the more obscure scientific symbols such as the 'approximately equals sign' or the chemical equilibrium symbol. Perhaps I should add a warning that creating your own character set is a pretty tedious and time-consuming process.

Pitch
Pitch is the number of characters per inch (cpi); the usual value is either 10 or 12 cpi. Obviously the higher the pitch the greater the number of words you can fit on a page. However if you use a pitch much greater than 12 cpi, the text will appear cramped and be difficult to read. Daisywheel printers and matrix printers invariably offer a choice of pitch. With a daisywheel you have to set the pitch before printing while the matrix printers can often alter pitch under software control.

Spacing
In most character sets the letters have different widths: the 'w' is wider than the 'i' and the 'm' is wider than 'n' which is in turn wider than the 'l'. Unfortunately with most cheap printers, the narrow letters take up as much room as the wider ones. A printer claiming to support **proportional spacing** will space characters according to their true widths. Proportionally spaced text is very pleasing to the eye and has a very professional appearance. Some printers offer **incremental spacing** where the printer is able to 'print' spaces as narrow as 120th of an inch. As the text arrives from the computer, the printer calculates how many complete words it can fit onto the current line. Each character is allocated the same amount of space, but the printer spaces the **words** evenly across the page. The printer is able to achieve such precise intra-word spacing because it is able to work with spaces as small as 120th of an inch.

However, you must understand that your word processor has to be able to take advantage of such sophisticated features. The present version of Quill does not support either proportional or incremental spacing.

Superscripts, subscripts and underlining
The majority of daisywheel printers and some matrix printers now support superscripts, subscripts and underlining. Underlining with cheap matrix printers is either impossible or it produces such wretched looking text that is is inadvizable to use the feature.

Different character sizes
The more advanced dot-matrix printers offer a variety of character sizes: **condensed** text, **double-width** characters and **double-height** characters. Condensed text usually leads

to pretty illegible text since the printer crams upwards of 132 characters into the space normally allotted to 80 characters. It is suitable for draft documents and it does economize on expensive paper. The condensed text option becomes especially useful with financial spreadsheets like Abacus where you often need lines of up to 180 characters.

Double-height and double-width characters are especially good for headings and titles. Once again expanded text is not aesthetically very pleasing but it is an option well worth having.

Printer speeds

One of the first psychological effects of using a computer is that it distorts your sense of time. So many things happen virtually instantaneously on a computer, that to wait say 10 seconds for a program to load can seem like an eternity. Therefore in choosing a printer, high speed is not just important in terms of efficiency but also it helps in maintaining your sanity! Consider carefully the minimum print speed which will meet your needs.

A typical daisywheel printer will print between 15 and 50 characters per second (cps). Matrix printers can go much faster and it is not unusual to find speeds of up to 150 cps quoted. However you should treat all manufacturer's speed ratings with a certain amount of scepticism. Most people are familiar with the so-called urban-cycle mpg statistics for petrol consumption in motor cars. With a number of reservations, we accept them as a useful indicator of the actual petrol consumption we might expect from a new car. Manufacturer's printer speed ratings are more akin to motorway driving than to driving around town. The 'urban cycle' for printers includes not just printing characters, but also processing line-feeds, producing bold text, underlining, etc. For a real document, the print speed may be considerably slower than what you might have been led to believe from the manufacturer's specification.

Let us try and put these print speeds in some sort of perspective. A typical A4 page will contain about 450 words (2700 characters – average 6 characters per word). A typist working at 50 words per minute will complete such a page in 7 minutes. A dot-matrix printer will print the page in about 1 minute. In fact if the printer actually approximates to 80 cps, it will finish the page in half a minute; 14 times faster than the typist and without any mistakes!

Matrix printers are not only faster than daisywheel printers they often offer a far wider choice of print speeds. This flexibility is useful: you can print draft documents at high speed when print quality is not critical, and then revert to a slower speed for near-letter print when the document is finished.

A fast printer is absolutely essential for business applications. Even in a small business, the monthly printing of accounts and invoices can take a reasonably fast printer many hours to complete. The most prudent assumption to make when choosing a printer is that your present printing needs are less than they will be in the future. Therefore select a printer that is faster than your existing requirements.

Noise and vibration
Printers are mechanical devices and they make a noise. Some of them make a lot of noise! There are types of printers on the market that run silently: thermal and ink-jet printers. However I don't consider they represent a practical proposition for word processing at their present stage of technical development.

In general the greater the printing speed the louder the noise. There is no standard way of measuring printer noise, so manufacturers either claim that their printers are 'quiet' or they make no claims, in which case you can safely assume they are going to be pretty noisy. Obviously a retail shop is not the ideal environment to estimate how noisy a printer may be. I would not recommend asking everybody in the shop to keep quiet while you try to listen to a printer! Instead express your anxiety about noise to the salesman and see if suitable arrangements can be made for you to hear the printer in quieter surroundings.

It is vital not to underestimate the noise produced by printers. You will find it extremely irritating if you have to switch off the printer to make a phone call or to conduct a conversation below the threshold of pain! It is possible to purchase 'acoustic-hoods' for daisywheel printers. These do smother the noise every effectively but have the drawback of being both very bulky and quite expensive.

Noise and vibration tend to go hand-in-hand. Daisywheel printers are much heavier than matrix printers and when they are going full out they can make a normal office desk resonate quite badly. I know of at least one office where the printer is kept on the floor – even a daisywheel printer can't shake the foundations of a building.

It is not advizable to place a computer on the same surface as a noisy, vibrating printer. It is not unknown for the integrated circuits to become dislodged inside the computer. Dampening vibration is a really intractable problem, but you might try a foam rubber mat or even a thick blanket. If you do experiment along these lines be careful not to block any cooling vents that might be on or near the bottom of the printer. Special stands are available to house daisywheel printers and these are probably the best solution. However they do take up a lot of room and they will involve you in additional expenditure.

Bidirectionality
Some printers are designed to print from right to left as well as from left to right. This increases the speed of printing since the printhead does not have to waste time returning to the left margin before restarting printing.

Contrary to what you might think, bidirectional printers are not twice as fast as normal printers. You should treat the manufacturer's claims with scepticism since in practice the time saved is fairly marginal. One estimate put the time saved at about 4%. Of course if you do a large amount of printing this may represent a significant saving of time.

Logic-seeking
Logic-seeking is a nice fancy term to describe 'intelligent' bidirectional printing. The printhead in bidirectional printing sweeps backwards and forwards across the full width of the paper regardless of where the text is on the page. For example, if there is a column of text in the centre of the page, the printhead will still oscillate between the edges of the page. A logic-seeking printer 'knows' where the text is to be printed and only moves as far along a line as is necessary to print the text.

Buffers
In order to print in both directions a printer needs to store temporarily the line that is to be printed on the backwards pass. This text is stored in a **print buffer**. Most printers have some kind of print buffer; the size varies from between 256 characters (3 or 4 lines) to 2 or 3 thousand characters (a typical A4 page). The larger the buffer, the less time a computer spends idling away waiting to send the next block of text.

A computer is capable of churning out text much more quickly than the speed of even the fastest printer. In order to overcome this mismatch of speeds the computer and the printer need to engage in some form of dialogue. When the print buffer is nearly full, the printer tells the computer to suspend sending characters while it prints the text in the buffer. As the buffer empties, the printer sends a message to the computer, informing it that it is now ready to receive more text. The jargon for this dialogue is **handshaking**.

There are three standard ways for computers and printers to communicate. The first is the simplest and is used by the QL. When the buffer is nearly full, the printer changes the

voltage on one of the wires in the print cable. The computer
is continually monitoring this voltage and as soon as it
detects a voltage change it stops sending text. When the
printer is ready to receive text again, it restores the original
voltage on the line. Once again the computer picks up this
signal and re-starts transmission.

XON/XOFF
The second method is for the printer to send special
characters XON and XOFF to control the flow of data.
When the computer receives an XOFF character it ceases
transmission and only restarts on the receipt of an XON
character.

ACK/ETX
The final method is similar to the XON/OFF approach. The
computer sends a fixed number of characters that can fit
into the buffer of the printer. This block of text is terminated
by a special character called ETX. The printer continues to
print text until it meets the ETX code. The ETX code
signifies to the printer that it has completed that block of
text and it requests more data by sending an ACK character
back to the computer. The receipt of the ACK code is a cue
to the computer to send the next block of characters.

XON/OFF and ACK.ETX are known as **communication
protocols** and we shall meet them again when we discuss
data communications. Quill at present does not support
communication protocols.

**Paper
handling**
On your journey to buy your printer stop off at your local
stationers and look at the range of merchandise on display:
different size paper (A4, A5, A3, etc.), continuous forms,
envelopes, labels, letterhead paper, etc. Pause a moment
and consider what kind of stationery you are likely to use in
the future. Your deliberations will help to determine what
kind of printer you should buy.

There are two methods of feeding paper into a printer:
friction-feed and **traction (sprocket) feed**. A friction-feed
mechanism is identical to the paper feed on a typewriter.
Essentially the paper is moved through the printer by the
friction between the paper and the roller (platen). This
method is ideal for single sheets of paper but problems can
occur with fanfold paper. Normal wear and tear on the
roller leads to a slightly uneven paper feed which is
unimportant for a single sheet but the error accumulates on
a long print run.

The cheapest and most convenient type of paper is
continuous-feed paper often known as fanfold paper. This
paper has sprocket holes running down each edge.

Normally the edges are perforated to enable the sprocket holes to be stripped off. Expensive brands of fanfold paper have very fine perforations which result in a much smoother edge than with the cheaper brands. The paper comes in wide variety of sizes, the most common being 9½ by 11 inches. Once the sprocket holes have been removed it measures 8½ by 11 inches, which is the standard A4 size.

A tractor-feed mechanism uses the sprocket holes on the fanfold paper. The paper is clamped on to two tractor wheels attached to the printer. As the tractor wheels rotate, they pull the paper through the printer. This process results in a smooth, even paper flow through the printer.

In theory a friction-feed printer should be able to cope with continuous stationery by simply ignoring the sprocket holes. However, for the reasons outlined above, this is not a very reliable approach. On the other hand tractor-feed printers cannot cope with single sheets of paper, envelopes, or your normal business forms unless they have been preprinted on fanfold paper. If you are likely to do a lot of single-sheet printing you might consider purchasing a single-sheet feeding device. These automatically insert a single sheet into the printer; otherwise you have to feed the sheets in by hand which is both tiresome and prone to error.

A number of printers offer both types of feed mechanism and it is well worthwhile having this flexibility – if you can afford the extra cost.

Finally, a warning about the use of **sticky labels** in printers. The labels have a tendency to become detached from the backing paper and then literally gum up the feed mechanism. As you might guess they always get stuck in the most inaccessible part of the machine. You need to be a qualified engineer to dismantle some machines in order to remove the labels. Sometimes a liberal dose of methylated spirits will prise them loose but it is not a practice I would recommend. If you intend to use a lot of sticky labels then make sure your printer allows easy access to the relevant parts of the feed mechanism.

Reliability

The bad news is that printers do break down; the good news is that it does not seem to happen very frequently. Although printers are mechanical devices, they seem remarkably resilient compared to other so-called consumer durables. If they do develop a fault, nine times out of ten it will be the mechanical components not the electronics. The drive mechanism and the printhead appear most susceptible to wear and tear.

Nevertheless it will be out of order occasionally and you

must plan for such an eventuality. It is only prudent to take out a service and maintenance contract for your printer especially if it is going to be heavily used.

There is no agreed method for measuring the reliability of printers; nor is there a handy *Which* report to help you identify any rogue brands. It is possible to gather a lot of information about particular brands from reading magazine reviews and talking to printer dealers. It is hardly a scientific procedure but there is no practical alternative.

Summary

Let us recap on the equipment you will need when you visit your friendly printer dealer:

● The QL to ensure it is compatible with the printer.
● A magnifying glass to study the true descenders and the dottiness of the characters.
● A noise meter to see if you will need ear plugs to use it.
● A vibration meter to test if it will shake the cups off the shelf.
● Sundry bits of paper to see if it actually prints on the stuff.
● A stop-watch to measure the speed.
● A ruler to measure the proportional and incremental spacing.
● A screwdriver to see if it is easy to dismantle to get at the stuck labels.
● A hammer to test if it will withstand normal wear and tear and, of course, save money!

I misled you at the start of this chapter when I said that purchasing a printer would give you headaches. It is more likely to be migraine. Good Luck!

Chapter 3

AN OVERVIEW OF WORD PROCESSING

What is a word processor?

I have a confession to make: I do not know how to answer this question. Dozens of definitions exist but somehow they all seem so unsatisfactory. Consider this definition: '. . . a word processor is a typewriter with memory'. It reminds me of the 19th Century description of the motor car as a 'horseless carriage'. A quaint definition but in retrospect it hardly conveys the tremendous impact of the motor car on society. The American National Standards Institute defines word processing as the 'transformation of ideas and information into a readable form of communication through the management of procedures, equipment and personnel'. I am sure writing that made them feel better, but are we any the wiser after reading it? It is futile to try to define word processing. Let us move on and discover why word processing is about to revolutionize our methods of communication.

The need

The typewriter is one of the most familiar objects in any office or home. Yet for many people, using a typewriter is comparable to a visit to the dentist. The more important the document they need to type – the greater the anxiety. The same ritual is performed every day all around the world: the paper is collected – always more than one sheet even if the text is to be only 5 lines long; the erasing fluid is found; the ribbon is tested for smudging and then finally the drudgery of typing begins. A mistake makes you reach for the Tippex; a mispelled word tortures you with questions: 'Shall I abandon this page?', 'Will anybody notice ?', 'Surely one error is acceptable'; an omitted phrase leads to a crumpled bundle in the bin. Once the document is typed merely to contemplate redrafting induces a state of depression.

If you think I am exaggerating then listen to the experience of William Boyd who was runner-up for the prestigious 1982 Booker McConnell Prize for Fiction. Recently he gave a very revealing picture of a writer's life. After reflecting on his obsession with writing in pencil he describes his attitude to typing. 'I hate typing . . . My original manuscript is so riddled with deletions, insertions, second, third and fourth thoughts, etc., that it is illegible to all but me. But I preferred the burden of a fair copy (in pencil) to the purgatory of weeks at a typewriter.' This sort of experience is no longer necessary; the purgatory of weeks at a typewriter could so easily be replaced by the heaven of a few days on a word processor.

The advantages

Quill has all the features you need to make the experience described above a thing of the past. You no longer need to be a good typist because correcting errors is so ridiculously easy. Inserting or deleting a character is accomplished with at most a couple of keystrokes. If you notice you have omitted a word, you simply move to the appropriate spot on the screen and type it in. The word processor automatically adjusts the text to incorporate the additional word. No one would ever be able to detect that a correction had been made. Contrast this process with the mess produced by using correcting fluid. Also a word processor allows you to insert additional lines or, if necessary, chop lines out.

The few features described above would be sufficient incentive for most two-fingered typists to rush out and buy a word processor! However we have not even begun to explore the real power of word processors. Quill also permits you to delete a word, part of a line, a paragraph, a whole page and if necessary a complete document. In fact you can do some pretty drastic surgery on your text in just a few seconds unless you are careful.

Moving around your text

Have you ever considered why books are so convenient to use? You may browse through the pages in either direction; you may move instantly to either the first or last page; providing the pages are numbered, you can go more or less directly to a specific page. In computer jargon books display many of the characteristics of a random-access device. In other words, to reach a particular page it is not necessary to read all the preceding pages.

A good word processor compares favourably with a book in terms of ease of moving about a text. Quill, for example, enables you to move:

- a character to the left or right
- a line up or down
- to the first page
- to the last page
- to a specified page

If you wish to browse through the text then just keep your finger on the cursor down key. When you attempt to push the cursor off the bottom of the screen you will see a fresh line of text appear at the bottom line. The rest of the text moves up and the top line disappears off the top of the screen. Relax, the line is not lost forever. If you now reverse this procedure by attempting to move the cursor beyond the top of the screen, the top line reappears and the bottom line disappears again. Using the cursor in this way it is possible to move smoothly through a whole document. This method of moving through the text is called **scrolling**.

Cut and paste   You have the similar degree of freedom in entering text. There is virtually no restriction on the way you can insert additional text into an existing document. Move the cursor to the appropriate place in the text and start typing. If you wish to insert a word, a phrase, a line, a paragraph, a page or even twenty pages, it makes absolutely no difference. The additional text will be incorporated automatically into your document.

Rearranging the order of text in a document by literally cutting it up and sticking it back together again is so common that the phrase 'cutting and pasting' has been coined to describe the process. With a word processor you store away your scissors and glue forever. Imagine I want to move this paragraph to, say, the beginning of this chapter. Although the details may differ the method used by most word processors is broadly the same: specify the text to be moved, specify its eventual destination and then give the **MOVE** command. It is as simple as that. The text is erased from its present position and transferred to the location you have specified. Occasionally you may wish to repeat the same passage in different parts of your document. The procedure is essentially the same except this time you issue the **COPY** command.

If you wish you may type your paragraphs in random order and subsequently rearrange them into the correct order. It would be like fitting the pieces of a jigsaw together to complete a picture. Naturally I am not advocating this procedure as a style of writing!

Search and replace

Most of us have a 'mental block' when it comes to the spelling of particular words. I simply cannot spell the word successful (I hope that is correct). Suppose you have consistently mispelled the word 'successful' as 'sucessful' throughout a large document. With a conventional typed manuscript, you would have no option but to scan each page looking for the mispelled word. Quill has a powerful 'search and replace' command which will find all instances of the incorrect spelling and then replace them with the correct spelling.

Ironically the sheer power of a word processor militates against it being used efficiently. Consider the 'search and replace' command; it has many other applications over and above correcting spelling mistakes. Suppose you are writing an article about word processing. While creating your manuscript you could substitute the abbreviation 'wp' for the phrase 'word processor'. Prior to printing the document, you invoke the search and replace command and you replace all instances of 'wp' with word processor. You might consider developing your own form of short-hand for writing documents. The prospect of combining the speed of shorthand typing with the overall power of a word processor is truly mind-boggling.

Form letters

The public relations industry has managed to achieve the impossible: the impersonal 'personalized' letter. I am sure you know the sort of letter I am talking about. Despite the 'Dear Mr or Mrs So and So' at the start, you know full well that thousands of other people are reading exactly the same letter across the nation. These 'form letters' were one of the first major applications of word processors. Presumably the marketing departments are right in assuming that we are flattered by this 'personal touch' in their correspondence. If you are a small businessman, then you may wish to use a similar technique in your business communications. Some word processors include a 'form letter' facility as an integrated part of the package. Unfortunately the present version of Quill does not provide such an option although I believe it is likely to be included in a future upgrade.

The form letter illustrates the ability of a word processor to combine text from different files: a name and address file and a letter file. Merging text from separate files allows you to eliminate much repetitive typing. A sample of any business's correspondence will show that similar phrases and paragraphs are being typed and retyped every day:

'We regret that the goods . . . are presently out of stock.
We expect to have a delivery . . .'

'Thank you for your inquiry . . .'

To minimize such repetitive typing a business may resort to printing standard letters. The secretary then fills in the gaps left in the letter with the details relating to that particular customer. These letters often look very unprofessional: invariably the typeface used by the secretary is different to the typeface used in the body of the letter. Also it takes time to position the paper correctly so that the added words are aligned properly with the existing text. Anyway the customer *knows* he has received a standard letter and the attempt to personalize it is almost certainly self-defeating.

A word processor solves this problem in an especially elegant way. It enables you to create and store your commonly used paragraphs as separate files on your Microdrive. When the time comes to type a letter you simply call up the appropriate paragraphs and they are inserted into the text. At this moment the typist is also able to remove some of those irritating phrases so common in standard letters: 'delete where applicable' . . . Frequently it is possible to dispense with those notorious covering letters. Often these letters merely reflect the reality that the world is full of standard letters to non-standard customers. A word processor allows you to integrate the points you wish to make in the covering letter into the main body of the 'standard' letter.

On-screen formatting

Albert Einstein is quoted as saying: 'I know why there are so many people who love chopping wood. In this activity one immediately sees the results.' Substitute the phrase 'word processing' for wood in this quote and you have one reason why word processing is so satisfying. The screen shows a faithful image of the final printed document.

It is not unusual to see a hand-written manuscript covered in so-called printer's marks. The printing trade has devized a special set of graphical symbols that a writer uses, as a form of shorthand, to tell a typist or printer how to lay out their document. For example you may wish to specify the size of margins, the spacing between lines, whether a particular word is to be underlined, etc. A word-processing program like Quill makes printers' marks virtually redundant. It has the capability to format your text before it is printed. As the Sinclair advertising brochure for Quill crudely states: 'You see what you get'.

The jargon for this facility is 'on-screen formatting'. Quill has an extensive range of formatting commands. Here are just a few to give you a flavour of what is available to you.

All of the commands will be explained in a later chapter.

- **Line spacing:** single, double or triple
- **Margins:** left, right, top and bottom
- **Tabs:** left, right, centre and decimal
- **Typeface:** bold, underlined, superscript and subscript
- **Running text:** headers, footers and page numbers

Saving your hard work

While you are typing your text the characters are being stored in the memory of the QL. If there is a power failure not only will the lights go out, but the QL will 'crash' and you will lose all the text. This is by way of being a dramatic reminder to you that until you save your text onto a Microdrive, it is very vulnerable to being lost. All word processors allow you to store documents permanently on either a floppy disk or a Microdrive.

Writing with a word processor

In the sections above, I have been discussing what might be called the mechanical advantages of using a word processor. After you have been using a word processor for some time you will notice that there are other, more intangible, benefits. You will notice that your whole attitude to writing changes. You begin to realize what all professional writers already know, that good writing is a process of thinking, writing, revizing and revizing until your deadline. Now you concentrate on polishing the text rather than focusing on the finished product – the typed document.

One measure of the quality of a word processor is the extent to which using it interferes with the thinking process. The user should be able to use the commands almost without thinking. If the user is uncertain about the function of a particular command help should be instantly available on screen. It is a sign of a good word processor if the manual is able to gain dust on the shelf. If you find that you are constantly having to look in the manual then buy yourself another word processor!

Arthur C. Clarke writes that: 'Any sufficiently advanced technology is indistinguishable from magic'. Let's get on and use Quill to see what he means!

Chapter 4

GETTING STARTED AND SIMPLE EDITING

Loading Quill

After you have switched on the QL, you will be asked to specify whether you are using a monitor or an ordinary television. If you indicate that you have a monitor, then text will be displayed in lines of 80 characters. Otherwise the QL will display lines of 64 characters which is the maximum line length that can be displayed satisfactorily on a TV.

A flashing cursor on the left-hand side of the screen signifies that the QL is awaiting a command. You have a number of things to do before you load and run Quill:

● Make the Quill cartridge 'read-only' by snapping off the plastic tab from the side of the cartridge. This will be your 'master' cartridge. In a moment I will show you how to make a duplicate copy of this cartridge. You should only use your master to make backup copies of Quill. Snapping off the tab will prevent Quill from being accidentally erased or overwritten.

● Format a blank cartridge which can then be used to store your text files. You may format a cartridge from within Quill but it is easier to format cartridges from SuperBASIC. One point you should note is that you must always have a formatted cartridge in Microdrive 2 when you are using Quill. The procedure for formatting a cartridge is as follows:

a) Insert the blank cartridge in the *right-hand* drive
b) Type in the format command:

　　　format MDV2__test__dat

MDV2 is the device name for the right-hand Microdrive; **test__dat** is an arbitrary name assigned to the cartridge to give an indication of the type of data stored on the cartridge. A cartridge containing a membership list might be called 'members_dat'; accounting data might be stored on a cartridge called 'accounts_dat', etc. You cannot store data on a cartridge until it has been formatted.

● If you have not yet made a duplicate copy of Quill, do it now! Place the cartridge containing Quill in the right-hand drive, the blank cartridge in the left-hand drive, and then run the following program:

lrun MDV1_clone

Remove the duplicate copy of Quill and format another blank cartridge to store your text files. Now remove your 'master' Quill cartridge and store it in a safe place. In future you will use the copy of Quill that you have just made.

The cartridge containing Quill has been programmed to **auto-boot** (auto-run) Quill. This means that you do not need to give a specific command to load and run Quill. All you have to do is switch on the QL and then insert the cartridge in the first drive. Quill will be automatically loaded and run. Remember that you must never insert a cartridge *before* switching on the QL.

Auto-booting   The system for auto-booting programs is very straightforward: after you have switched on the QL and identified the type of VDU you are using, the QL immediately searches the cartridge in drive 1 for a file called **boot_bas**. This file contains an instruction to the QL to load and run Quill. On the cartridge containing Easel, 'boot_bas' contains an instruction to load and run Easel. If you wish you may use this technique to auto-run some of your own programs. There are some disadvantages in having Quill auto-run each time, so if you wish to stop it auto-booting in future you could rename 'boot_bas' to 'quillgo_bas'. When you wish to run Quill in future you enter:

lrun MDV1_quillgo_bas

Normally you will run Quill by using the auto-boot facility. Why didn't Quill auto-run on this occasion? Because the Quill cartridge was not in drive 1 at the appropriate time. If you want to see this auto-boot facility in action, remove the cartridges and then switch the QL off and then back on again. Place the Quill cartridge in drive 1 and the blank cartridge in drive 2. Answer the question about your VDU and then you will see Quill automatically loaded and run.

Figure 4.1   The QL opening screen with choice of monitor or TV

Figure 4.2   Loading Quill

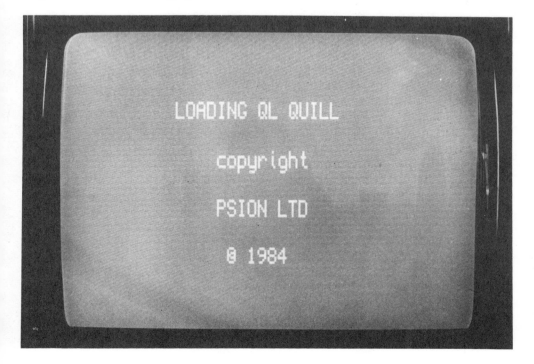

In fact if the QL is already switched on, then the fastest way to run Quill is to press the **reset** button. As I explained in Chapter 1, pressing the reset button makes the QL act as if it has just been switched on. Using the reset button saves you having to go to your wall-plug to switch the machine off.

While Quill is being loaded into the QL you should see the small light adjacent to drive 1 become illuminated. This **LED** is switched on every time the QL accesses a Microdrive. After a few seconds the Psion logo appears momentarily on the screen to be replaced quickly by the main Quill screen. Before you start entering any text, examine the screen carefully.

The main Quill screen

The screen is divided into four sections: **control area, ruler, display area** and **status area**.

Control area
At the top is the control area which I shall refer to as the **menu**. It functions very much like the menus you see in Chinese take-away restaurants. To make it easier for

Figure 4.3   Formatting a cartridge

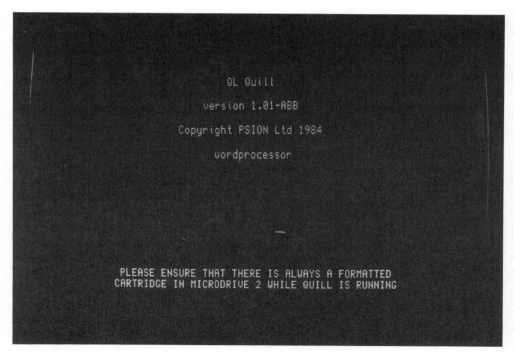

QL Quill

version 1.01-ABB

Copyright PSION Ltd 1984

wordprocessor

PLEASE ENSURE THAT THERE IS ALWAYS A FORMATTED
CARTRIDGE IN MICRODRIVE 2 WHILE QUILL IS RUNNING

Figure 4.4   Inserting the Quill cartridge

Figure 4.5   The main Quill screen

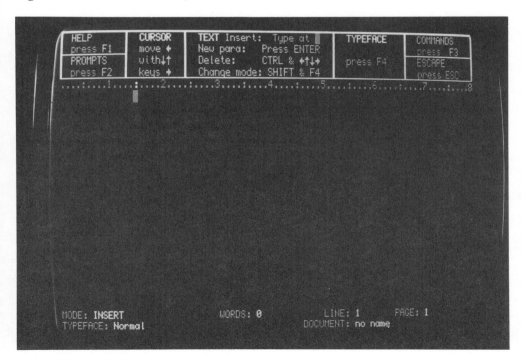

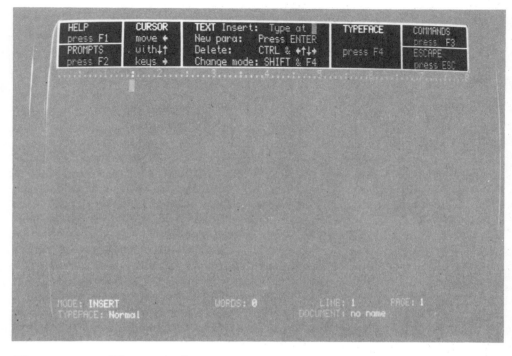

Figure 4.6   The control area

Figure 4.7   The ruler

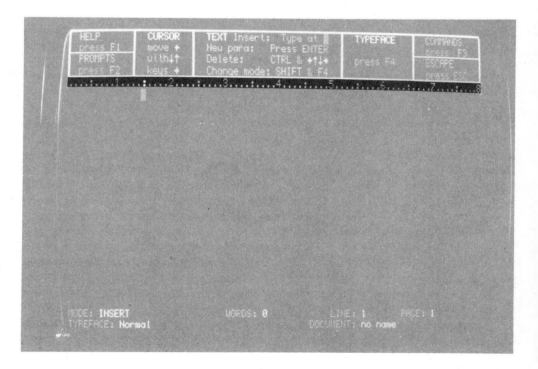

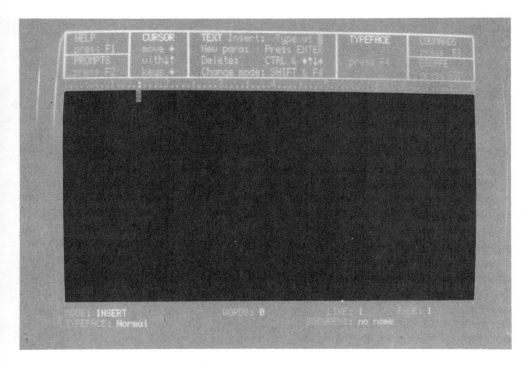

Figure 4.8   The display area

Figure 4.9   The status area

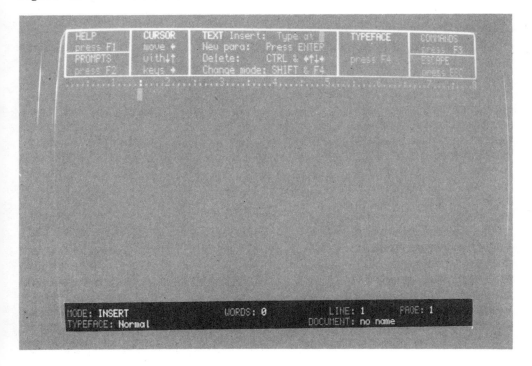

customers to select dishes they probably can't pronounce, each dish is allocated a number so that selecting your dishes is reduced to listing the numbers of the dishes you want. A Quill menu works in a very similar fashion: for example, if you want to select a command you merely press F3; you are not required to type in the word 'commands'.

Ruler
— :— 1— : — 2 —:— 3 — : — 4 — : —5 —:— 6—

Just below the menu is a dotted line called the ruler. Counting from the left, at every fifth position is a colon (:) and at every tenth position is a number. At the beginning of a Quill session you will see the cursor positioned directly below the '1' in the ruler. The '1' signifies that the cursor is at the tenth character position on the line. If it was under the '2', it would be in the twentieth column. The main function of the ruler is to give you a visual, numeric guide to the current location of the cursor on the screen.

Display area
Below the ruler is the display area which is where the text you enter will be displayed.

Status area
Finally the last three lines on the screen are reserved as the status area.

Menu choices

Mode
At the top left-hand corner of this area are the words MODE: INSERT. I shall explain in a later section the significance of the word INSERT; for the time being it is sufficient for you to know that Quill has two modes: INSERT and OVERWRITE. To change from one mode to the other, you press the SHIFT and F4 keys. The word OVERWRITE now appears alongside MODE. Repeat the same keystrokes and INSERT appears alongside MODE. Repeat the same keystrokes and INSERT reappears. How will you remember this command? You don't need to; it is one of the commands on the menu! The menu option I am referring to is:

Change Mode SHIFT key and F4

SHIFT F4, like many other commands in Quill, acts as a toggle. A toggle may be likened to a light switch. If you press the switch when the light is on, it turns it off. If the light is off, pressing the switch turns it on. SHIFT F4 toggles between INSERT and OVERWRITE mode. Be careful to press SHIFT before F4 otherwise it will be treated as a Typeface command.

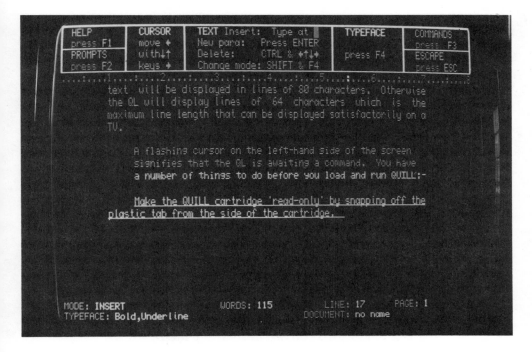

Figure 4.10   Using bold and underline

Typeface
Quill can underline text, produce boldface text, and generate superscripts and subscripts. If you are using any of these special features, you will see them listed alongside Typeface. The typeface command is F4. For example:

TYPEFACE: UNDERLINE
TYPEFACE: BOLD, UNDERLINE

Words
The number alongside Words represents a running count of the words in the document. A word is any string of characters terminated by a space or tab character.

Line and page
If you have not typed in any text, the cursor will be on page 1 and line 1. The line and page information is constantly changed as you move the cursor around a document.

Document
Opposite Document is the name of the file you are currently editing. Because you have not yet given the file a name, Quill temporarily assigns the filename 'no name' to the file. You will be prompted to assign a filename of your own choice when you save the file onto a cartridge.

Simple editing

You will need some text to make the following discussion more meaningful. I would recommend that you now type in the sample text shown in Exercise 1 below, as I will be constantly referring to this text in future sections. Before you start typing please bear the following points in mind:

- Type in the document as if you were using a typewriter.

- Where you see <ENTER>, press the **ENTER** key. But do not, *repeat*, do not hit the ENTER key except where you see it is marked on the text.

- If you make a mistake you can press **CTRL** and ← together to delete the last character you typed in.

- The text includes a number of deliberate mistakes (marked in bold text). Resist the temptation to correct them as you go along. Later on we will use them for practising Quill's editing commands. Don't worry if you inadvertently make mistakes that you don't know how to correct. The important point is to include my mistakes; your mistakes are unimportant.

- Make sure you are in INSERT mode.

- The text on your screen may look slightly different to the text of Exercise 1. It will depend on whether you are using a monitor or television. I created this text using a television with lines of 64 characters.

Exercise 1

If you haven't already done so, enter the text shown below.

A SAMPLE TEXT WITH DELIBERATE MISTAKES
<ENTER>
EXAMPLE TEXT <ENTER>
<ENTER>
TYPING <ENTER>

Using Quill to type docu**mmm**ents is so easy and quick because it is juist like typing one continuous line. If you are an experienced typist, **itwill** sometimes be difficult to conatrol the reflex to press **press** the ENTER key at the end of each line. The only time you need to press the ENTER key is at the end of each paragraph. <ENTER>.
    Correcting **correcting** errors which is a nightmare when using a typewriter is amazingly simple using QUAIL. You have such a wide choiyce of commands that the main problem **problem** is selecting the most efficient one.
<ENTER>

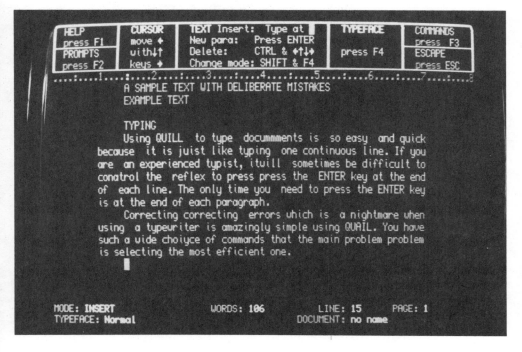

Figure 4.11 Main Quill screen with Exercise 1 typed in

Moving the cursor
After typing in Exercise 1, the cursor will be positioned in
the 10th column in the line below the text. The four
arrowed keys allow you to move the cursor around the text.
Move the cursor to the middle of the text using the ↑ key
and then experiment with the four cursor keys.

No-go areas   When you are satisifed that you understand
how the cursor keys work, move the cursor as far down the
screen as you can. You will discover that the cursor meets
an invisible wall just below the end of the text. Now try to
move the cursor beyond the top of the screen. Once again
you will find that it is impossible to move the cursor outside
of the text area. Why? The explanation is very simple: the
cursor keys move about the text area. You must not make
the mistake of treating the display area as being
synonymous with the text area. It is only possible to move
the cursor to the characters you typed in. The blank part of
the screen below the text does not contain any text
characters. A blank screen is not the same as a screen-full of
spaces!

Soft and hard spaces   Now move the cursor slowly along
any line of text. Study carefully how the cursor moves
between words. You will see the cursor appear to jump

over spaces between the words. There are two kinds of spaces in your text: 'hard' and 'soft'. You generate a hard space everytime you press the space bar. Soft spaces are the spaces inserted by Quill to produce the straight right-hand margin. It is not possible to move the cursor to a soft space. This is why the cursor seems to hop along the lines; it is skipping over all the soft spaces.

Word wrap

As you typed in Exercise 1, you should have become acquainted with one of the most useful features of Quill: **word wrap**. Word wrap allows you to type in text without having to hit the ENTER key at the end of each line. When a word extends beyond the right margin, Quill automatically moves the *whole word* down to the beginning of the next line.

Soft and hard carriage returns   When Quill wraps the text around it inserts a **soft** carriage return and line-feed at the end of the line. In future I will use the term carriage return as short hand for carriage return and line-feed. Quill distinguishes between the soft carriage returns in inserts and the **hard** carriage returns that you insert when you press ENTER. In a moment we shall see how this distinction between hard and soft carriage returns alters the way in which Quill deletes text.

Typists will find the word wrap facility such a luxury. No longer will you have to listen out for the familiar warning bell that signifies that you are approaching the end of a line. Nor will you have to go through the tiresome process of calculating whether you can fit the next word on the end of the line. You can now let Quill handle the problem of fitting the words on the line and you can get on with typing your documents. The ENTER key is only used when you wish to force a break in a line, to create a blank line or to end a paragraph.

Blank lines

A blank line is not a line of spaces; it contains just two characters: a carriage return and a line feed. It is not possible to move the cursor along a blank line. If you try to do so, you will see the cursor jump to the beginning of the next line. To demonstrate this point, move the cursor to a blank line between 'example text' and 'typing' in Exercise 1. Now confirm that you cannot move along the line using the → key.

How would you insert the phrase 'blank line' starting at the 14th column of this blank line? Since it is not possible to move the cursor along the line, you will have to type 13 spaces followed by the phrase 'blank line'.

Deleting text: basic commands

The laws of natural justice never seemed to apply to me when I used a typewriter; making mistakes was so easy, correcting them so awfully difficult. Quill restores my faith in justice. It is imbued with a wonderful symmetry: eradicating errors is as easy as making them.

The commands for deleting text are shown on the menu:

DELETE CTRL KEY & ← ↑ ↓ →

We will begin by discussing the two commands for deleting single characters.

Deleting a single character   Exercise 1 has a number of mispelled words: docummments, juist, QUAIL and choiyce. Let us start by correcting docummments. Move the cursor to the middle 'm' in the word and then press CTRL and <. One 'm' immediately disappears and the cursor is now positioned over the first 'm'. CTRL and ← deletes the character to the *left* of the cursor. You could use the same procedure to delete another 'm' but first you would have to move the cursor to the second 'm'. It is faster to press CTRL and →. The 'm' *lying under* the cursor is removed and the cursor is now located over the remaining 'm'.

You may be asking why there are two commands to delete a single character? Before I answer this question let us distinguish clearly between them:

CTRL ←   deletes the character to the *left* of the cursor

CTRL →   deletes the character to the *right* of the cursor

If you keep the CTRL and ← keys depressed, you will see the cursor race up the screen devouring all the text in its path. While the same procedure with the CTRL and → keys causes the cursor to act like a black hole: the cursor remains stationary while the text below gets sucked relentlessly towards its doom.

Choosing which command to use will depend largely on *when* you notice that a mistake has been made. Imagine you are typing merrily away and you hit the wrong key. The most convenient way to eliminate the error is to immediately press CTRL and ←. However, suppose you only notice the error when you are further down the page. In this circumstance it is more 'natural' to move the cursor directly over the character you wish to delete and then hit the CTRL and → keys than to position the cursor to the left of the error and use the CTRL and ← keys.

Initially you may find using these two similar commands slightly confusing. However, if you persevere with both commands you will become accustomed to having them both at your disposal. I suggest you now practice both these

commands on the remaining misspelled words in
Exercise 1.

Inserting text
By now you will be fully aware of how easy it is to type in
text using Quill. The menu has the rather unhelpful prompt
'TEXT Type at' to indicate that text will always be inserted
at the location of the cursor.

Inserting extra text in the body of an existing document is
as easy as creating the document in the first place. You
simply move to the spot where you wish to enter additional
text and start typing. In the first paragraph of Exercise 1, a
space has been omitted between 'it' and 'will' (itwill). Move
the cursor to the 'w' and press the space bar. It is as easy as
that. Now let us insert the word 'very' between 'be' and
'difficult' in the same line. Move the cursor to the 'd' in
'difficult' and type 'very' *followed* by a space. Quill is so
flexible that you could if you wish insert a whole
paragraph, a page, or even forty pages at this point in the
text.

When you are inserting the odd character or word in a
text, you will see that Quill automatically adjusts the format
of the text as you make your alterations. However, if you try
to insert more than one word, you will suddenly see a gap
of two lines open up in front of the cursor. When Quill
detects that you are making a significant insertion of text, it
'decides' that it would be wasting its time and yours by
continually readjusting the format of the text. So it opens up
a reasonable space for additional text and this lets you get
on with your typing without the distraction of seeing the
text being continually reformatted. Quill will continue to
provide additional space until you signify that you have
ceased inserting extra text.

There are three ways to indicate that you have finished
inserting text:

1   Press any cursor.
2   Press any function key or the ESCape key.
3   Wait about ten seconds and Quill will assume that you
    have stopped entering text.

Quill automatically closes up the remaining gap at the end
of each insertion. The ten-second 'time-out' feature is very
annoying and it makes composing at the keyboard very
tiresome. To demonstrate how Quill handles insertions,
move to any point in Exercise 1 and type in a few lines of
gibberish. When you are satisfied that you understand the
mechanics of inserting text, use the delete commands to get
rid of the rubbish you have just typed in!

OVERWRITE mode INSERT mode signifies that everything you type will be **added** to the existing text. Sometimes however, you need to rewrite a section of text and not simply add some extra words or lines. For example in Exercise 1, you might wish to replace 'one continuous line' with 'a very long line'. Of course you could delete the words you don't want and type in the replacement text. But there is a more convenient and efficient method: OVERWRITE mode. Move the cursor to the 'o' in 'one' and then press SHIFT and F4. INSERT is immediately replaced by OVERWRITE in the status area. If you now type in the substitute passage you will see that the new text overwrites the old. OVERWRITE mode is a useful combination of delete and insert.

Because you will tend to be in INSERT mode most of the time, it is easy to get into the habit of ignoring OVERWRITE mode altogether. If you wish to use Quill efficiently, you should, from the very start, consciously look for opportunities to use OVERWRITE mode. Eventually you will appreciate that it is another valuable additional to the Quill reportoire of commands.

If you wish to return to INSERT mode hit SHIFT and F4 again.

Deleting text: further commands
So far we have discussed the two commands for deleting single characters. It is now time to meet the more advanced deletion commands available in Quill.

Deleting words SHIFT-CTRL→ will delete a whole word if the cursor is positioned on the first letter of the word. If you locate the cursor within the word, the command will delete all the characters from the cursor position to the end of the word. In this context it is acting as a delete-rest-of-word command.

As far as Quill is concerned, a word is any string of characters, including punctuation characters, that is followed by a space or tab. For example:

```
grape
grape,
grape-vine
grape.
```

are counted as single words.

The delete-word command is in some respects a misnomer. When you try to delete a whole word by positioning the cursor on the first letter, Quill will treat all the characters in the word *and* the subsequent spaces as the text to be deleted. If you think about this for a few moments, you will realize that Quill adopts the most sensible and efficient approach to the problem of deleting words. If Quill merely removed the characters that compose the word, then you would be left with superflous spaces in the text which would eventually have to be deleted by additional commands.

SHIFT-CTRL← is the symmetrical counterpart to the command described above: it deletes the word to the *left* of the cursor. Exercise 1 contains a number of duplicated words: 'press press', 'Correcting correcting' and 'problem problem'. Practise using these delete-word commands and pay special attention to the way Quill handles the following spaces.

Deleting parts of a line   Quill provides two further deletion commands which operate on sections of a line:

CTRL and ↑   deletes all the line to the *left* of the cursor.
CTRL and ↓   deletes all the characters from the cursor position to the end of the line.

You should note that the CTRL ↓ command not only deletes the rest of the text characters on the line but also the invisible *soft* carriage return at the end of the line. So you will see the text on the line below move up to fill the gap left by the deleted text. However CTRL ↓ will not delete a *hard* carriage return at the end of a line. The point I am trying to make is probably best clarified by an example.

Move the cursor to the 's' in 'sometimes' in the third line of paragraph 1 of Exercise 1. Hit CTRL and ↓ and you will see the line below move up to fill the gap left by the deleted text. This happens because there was a *soft* carriage return at the end of the line. Let us now use the same command on a line that was terminated by the ENTER key. Imagine you wanted the top line in Exercise 1 to contain the words 'A SAMPLE TEXT'. Move the cursor to the space after the word 'TEXT' and hit CTRL and ↓. The phrase 'WITH DELIBERATE MISTAKES' disappears as intended. But note that this time the line below was not moved up to fill the gap.

Deleting a whole line   There is no separate command to delete a complete line. You have two choices: you may move to the beginning of a line and use CTRL and ↓ or you can move to the end of a line and use CTRL and ↑. Of course you could achieve exactly the same effect by simply moving to anywhere on the line and using both the commands in succession.

Deleting blank lines   Earlier I explained that a blank line

actually consists of the carriage return and line-feed
characters. These characters may be deleted in exactly the
same fashion as any other text characters.

Move the cursor to a blank line, hit CTRL and → and the
line is removed. Another method is to move to the first
character on the line below a blank line and then press
CTRL and ←. If you have been paying attention you should
be doubtful as to whether these methods will actually work.
Both these commands delete a single character. A blank
line consists of two characters. Do they work?

Help

You may obtain information about any aspect of Quill by
calling up the on-line help files. Quill links the help files to
the command you are currently using. Imagine you had just
switched on OVERWRITE mode and you were unsure of its
function. If you call for help by pressing F1 you will be
shown the part of the help file that relates to OVERWRITE
mode.

Ironically, the help command does not tell you how to
exit from the help files and return to the main menu! You
press ESC to return to the main menu.

Figure 4.12   The help file

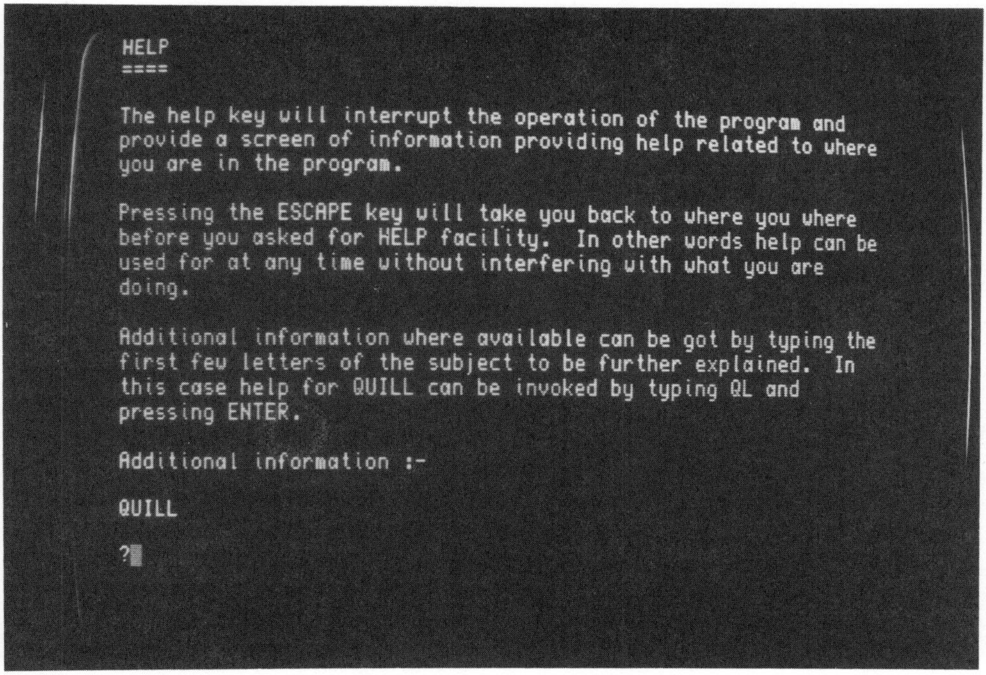

```
HELP
====

The help key will interrupt the operation of the program and
provide a screen of information providing help related to where
you are in the program.

Pressing the ESCAPE key will take you back to where you where
before you asked for HELP facility.  In other words help can be
used for at any time without interfering with what you are
doing.

Additional information where available can be got by typing the
first few letters of the subject to be further explained.  In
this case help for QUILL can be invoked by typing QL and
pressing ENTER.

Additional information :-

QUILL

?
```

Prompts   When you become proficient at using Quill, you will no longer need assistance from the menus. The menus reduce the amount of text that you can see on the screen. You may remove the menus from the screen by pressing F2, the PROMPTS command. F2 toggles the menus on and off.

Chapter 5

ADVANCED EDITING

We have now covered the basic methods for inserting and deleting text. It is now time to study some of the more advanced editing commands of Quill. However, before passing on to these commands it is necessary to extend our knowledge of Quill's cursor commands.

Further cursor commands

Word by word

The four cursor keys enable you to move character by character or line by line through a document. Moving one character at a time along a line of, say, 132 characters can be a pretty slow process.

Do not despair. Quill provides a much faster method of moving the cursor on a line:

SHIFT → moves the cursor *forward* one word at a time
SHIFT ← moves the cursor *back* in steps of one word

More precisely, SHIFT → moves the cursor to the first letter of the following word. It does not matter if the next word is on the line below, the cursor will still move to that word. SHIFT ← moves the cursor to the first letter of the preceding word. If the cursor is located in the middle of a word when you issue this command the cursor will move to the beginning of the word.

Paragraph by paragraph

SHIFT ↓ moves the cursor to the beginning of the next paragraph. SHIFT ↑ moves the cursor to the start of the preceding paragraph. If the cursor is in the body of a paragraph when this command is given, it will move to the beginning of that paragraph. These two commands will enable you to position the cursor at any point in a document extremely quickly.

If you press F3 as indicated in the top right-hand corner of the main menu, the screen will be transformed to show:

- The first command menu containing a partial list of the commands available.
- The word 'Command' which appears on the screen just above the normal status area.
- A second cursor displayed alongside 'Command'.

Quill has so many commands that it is impractical to include them all on one menu. The word OTHER in the command menu indicates that a further list of commands may be displayed by pressing 'O'. The commands are listed in alphabetical order in both menus. Commands beginning with the same letters have been placed on different menus, i.e.

Commands I	*Commands II*
FOOTER	FILES
HEADER	HYPHENATE
MARGIN	MERGE
PRINT	PAGE
SAVE	SEARCH

Command menus

The OTHER command toggles between the two command menus.

There are two kinds of commands in Quill:

- Commands requiring **two** keystrokes
- Commands requiring **three** keystrokes.

To use a command in the first menu, you need only two keystrokes: F3 followed by the first letter of the selected commands, e.g. F3 and M selects the MARGIN command. The commands in the second menu need three keystrokes: F3 O and the first letter of the command, e.g. F3 O M is the instruction to MERGE another Quill document into the document you are currently editing.

Please do not be deceived into thinking that the OTHER command is simply a way of looking at the two menus. The 'O' in OTHER is an integral part of the syntax of the commands on the second command menu, as shown in the example above. You might consider adopting the trick of regarding the second command menu as 'O' menu. I have a mental list of 'O' commands: **OF** – FILES, **OS** – SEARCH, etc. I have found this technique to be a useful way of avoiding the mistakes that can occur with commands that ostensibly start with the same letter.

You should be aware that it is possible to issue a command without waiting for the menus to appear. A reasonable typist will be able to type a command much faster than Quill can display the menus. Commands are

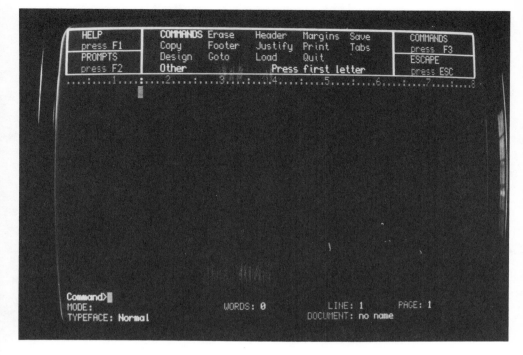

Figure 5.1   Quill screen with first command menu

Figure 5.2   Quill screen with second command menu

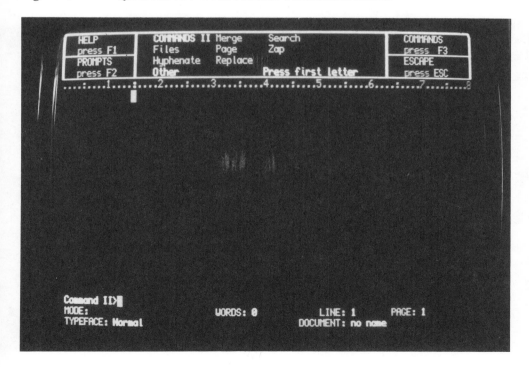

executed faster if Quill does not have to waste time displaying the menus.

The command line
While Quill displays the first command menu, the word Command will continue to be displayed on the line of the status area. I will refer to this line as the **command line**. If you call up the second menu, the command line changes to Commands II and this acts as a visual reminder that you are in the O menu. If you have switched off the menus by pressing F2, then the prompts in the command line serve as the only indicator of which command you are currently using. The prompts in the command line are superfluous if the menus are displayed.

The mysterious second cursor alongside the word Command is consistent with Quill's philosophy that a cursor always marks the location where the next character typed in will be displayed. Whenever you type in text as part of a command, it will be displayed in the command line, e.g. filenames in LOAD and SAVE commands. Press ESC to return to the main menu.

Editing the command line
The command line has its own set of cursor and editing commands so if you make a mistake when entering a command you do not need to abort the command.

←	moves one character to the *left*
→	moves one character to the *right*
SHIFT ←	moves one *word* to the left
SHIFT →	moves one *word* to the right
↑	moves to start of command line
↓	moves to end of command line
CTRL ←	deletes character to the left of the cursor
CTRL →	deletes character underneath cursor
CTRL ↑	deletes all command line to the left
CTRL ↓	deletes all command line to the right

GOTO
Our discussion of Quill's reportoire of cursor commands is completed with the **GOTO** command. This command enables you to proceed directly to either the top or bottom of a document. It gives you the option of jumping to the top of any specified page.

Press F3 and G and the command line displays GOTO. The menu offers you three options:

1   Hit T to go to the top of the document.
2   Hit B to move to the end (bottom) of the document.
3   Enter a page number if you wish to proceed to a particular page.

As soon as you hit either T or B, the cursor moves immediately to the top or bottom of the file respectively and you are automatically returned to the main menu. If you enter page number, say, 10 for example, then the command line changes to display GOTO, Page number, 10. Unlike with T and B you must hit ENTER before the command is executed. This gives you the opportunity to change your mind or correct the page number. Incidentally if you enter a number which is *less* than the lowest page number in the file, then the cursor moves to the top of the document. Similarly, if you enter a number which is *greater* than the highest page number in the file, then the cursor moves to the end of the document.

Suppose you have entered a page number but you decide instead that you actually wish to move to the top or bottom of the file. You may be tempted to try to delete back to the GOTO prompt. Well, it cannot be done. Quill allows you to delete the page number but not the page number prompt. However, if you hit ESC, you will be returned to the GOTO prompt and then you may press T or B in the normal way. This use of ESC is not really consistent with Quill's overall philosophy that the ESC key terminates or aborts a command and returns you to the main menu. It also means that to completely abort the GOTO command after you have entered a page number, you have to hit ESC twice.

This is probably an appropriate moment to list the full range of cursor commands:

←	moves one character to the *left*
→	moves one character to the *right*
SHIFT ←	moves one *word* to the left
SHIFT →	moves one *word* to the right
↑	moves *up* one line
↓	moves *down* one line
SHIFT ↑	moves up one *paragraph*
SHIFT ↓	moves down one *paragraph*
GOTO T	GOTO *top* of document
GOTO B	GOTO *bottom* of document
GOTO number	GOTO beginning of specified page

Finding text

Imagine you were told that a new kind of book had been invented that did not need an index. If you wish to locate a particular word or phrase in the book, you merely say the appropriate words and the book instantly opens at the relevant page. Such a wondrous book does not exist as far as I know, but Quill does exist and it can function in a very similar way to this imaginary book. With a few keystrokes you can use Quill to find one or all occurrences of a word or phrase in a document.

The SEARCH command

The procedure for searching through a document is very simple: it takes the form of dialogue between you and Quill. The command for searching through a document is **F3 OS**. The sequence of events is as follows:

1   Press F3 OS (the SEARCH command).

2   The command line appears and displays 'Search?'

3   The menu now prompts you to enter the text you wish to find. It is convenient to use the technical term **string** for the text you wish to find. The term string is commonly used in computing and you may as well become acquainted with it now. A string is literally any group of characters; for example this line is a string of characters.

4   Enter the string of characters you wish to find and then press ENTER. The search string will be displayed in the command.

5   'Searching? Accessing Microdrives' now appears in the command line.

6   If a match for your search string is found in the document, then the cursor is moved to that spot in the next.

7   'Continue?' is now displayed in the command line and the menu now offers you a choice of options. Press C to search for other occurrences of the string in the document. Press ESC to abandon the search. Repeated use of C will cause Quill to search through the whole document for every occurrence of your search string.

8   If no match for your string is found, then Quill displays

Not found – press any key to continue

in the command line and you are automatically returned to the main menu if you hit a key. The cursor returns to its original location before the search command was issued.

This question and answer form of dialogue is typical of most Quill commands and several general points are worth noting. Information about the execution of a command is displayed in two places: in the menu and in the command line. The menu changes at each stage of the command to indicate the range of options available. The command line keeps you informed of what Quill is doing, e.g. accessing Microdrives, searching, etc. It also displays a prompt which corresponds with the range of options shown in the menu. At first I found this very disconcerting. For example, in my early experiments with the SEARCH command, I found myself entering Y for Yes instead of C for Continue in response to the prompt 'Continue?' in the command line. This experience taught me a valuable lesson: when you are learning to use Quill concentrate on the menus, they are your guide to what to do next. The messages and prompts on the command line can be more or less ignored until you become more proficient in using Quill.

Several observations need to be made about the search command:

● Quill does not distinguish between upper and lower case letters in your search string. For example, suppose you wanted to search for the word 'line' in Exercise 1. You could type in line, LINE, LiNe or lINe as your search string and Quill would still match it to the word 'line' in the text. Of course this has advantages and disadvantages.

● The search command follows your instructions literally to the letter: if you tell it to find a string of characters it will find them in the text even if they are embedded in a long word. For example say you wanted to find the word 'time' in Exercise 1, you would see the cursor move instantly to the word some**times**. If you wanted to find 'time' as a whole word you would have to type in "time" as your search string. Even this approach is not completely satisfactory because you would miss 'time,', 'time.', etc.

● The most annoying feature of this command is that it immediately deletes the search string from the command line when it begins to search through the text. If no match is found for your string in the document then you have to consider two possibilities: the document does not contain the search string or the document does contain the string but you made a mistake in typing in the search string.

● Because you have no means of checking whether or not you typed in the search string correctly, you may have to repeat the command to make absolutely certain the string does not appear in the document. You will need to adopt the habit of carefully checking your search string before sending Quill off to find it.

The REPLACE command

Replacing one word or phrase for another throughout a document is a facility that no typewriter can offer. The **REPLACE** command enables you to move painlessly through a document exchanging one string for another.

Suppose you had just finished a hundred-page document

on Clive Sinclair. At the very last minute you are reminded that he was recently knighted and consequently all references to 'Clive Sinclair' need to be altered to 'Sir Clive Sinclair'. If you had used a typewriter for your document you would probably cry! Quill, however, solves the problem in a matter of seconds.

The procedure for restoring the lost knighthood is very simple and has a similar structure to the dialogue we discussed in connection with the SEARCH command. The REPLACE command is on the second command menu so you type **F3** and **OR**. The command line prompts you with 'Replace?' and the menu now asks you to type in the string you wish to replace. You type in 'Clive Sinclair' followed by ENTER. The cursor now moves immediately to the first occurrence of the string in the document. The command line changes to display 'with?' which is your cue to type in the replacement text 'Sir Clive Sinclair'. The menu now offers three options:

1   You may make the exchange by hitting R.
2   You may leave the text unchanged and ask Quill to search for further occurrences of the search string by pressing 'N' (Next occurrence).
3   You may abandon the command and return immediately to the main menu by hitting ESC.

If the string was not found at all or if there were no further occurrences of the string then Quill displays the message:

Not found – press any key to continue

The REPLACE command has essentially the same features as the SEARCH command: it will find and replace the search string even if it is contained in a longer string of text; it ignores the difference between upper and lower case letters; both the search and replacement strings are deleted from view as soon as you type them in. This command is in many ways much more powerful than the SEARCH command and requires correspondingly greater care in its use.

An intelligent use of the REPLACE command can save you a lot of typing. If you enter abbreviations for frequently used, long words and then replace them later with the full word it can save you a lot of time. For example, while typing in this text I used the abbreviation c★ for the word 'character'. Before sending the document off to the publishers I used the REPLACE command to substitute 'character' for all occurrences of c★.

The REPLACE command may be used for multiple deletions; for example if Sir Clive lost his knighthood for a treasonable act (like selling out to IBM!), you could delete all references to 'Sir' by entering "Sir" as the search string and simply hitting ENTER for the replacement string. This effectively tells Quill to replace 'Sir' with nothing or, in computerese, with the **null** string.

The COPY command

An essential feature of any word processor is the ability to copy or move a section of text from one place in a document to another. The jargon for this capability is **block** operations. A block is any continuous piece of text whose beginning and end has been marked in some way by the user. The size of the block may be one character, one line or even a complete document.

Quill's COPY command acts as a block move or block copy command depending on whether or not you decide to retain the original block. A **block move** is when you delete the original block. A **block copy** is when you keep the original block.

The COPY command is on the first command menu and is called by **F3** and **C**. The command line displays **Copy, start** and the menu asks you to move the cursor to where you wish the block to begin. As soon as you have positioned the cursor at the start of the block, hit ENTER. The command line now shows **Copy, end** and you are prompted to mark the end of the block by moving the cursor to the position in the text where you want the block to end. As you move the cursor you will see the text become highlighted. This highlighting defines the size of the block at any time. To mark the end of the block, press ENTER.

The command line now displays **Copy, copy** and the menu asks you to move the cursor to the location where you want the block inserted. When you press the R key, the block is inserted at the current position of the cursor.

The command line now prompts you with **Copy, keep** and Quill offers you the option of keeping or deleting the original block. If you press ENTER then the original block is retained. The original block is deleted if you press D.

Once you have the decision about deleting or retaining the original block, the command line reverts to **Copy, copy** again. You may, if you wish, make further copies of the block by moving the cursor to the selected locations and pressing ENTER. You should note that with these subsequent block insertions you are not offered the option of deleting the previous text inserted. If you do not wish to make further insertions press ESC.

Copy, start ↓	move to beginning of the block and mark it
Copy, end ↓	move to end of the block and mark it
Copy, copy ↓	insert block
Copy, keep ↓	now keep or delete original block
Copy, copy	make further copies or press ESC

The procedure for marking the end of a block seems so easy: move the cursor to the appropriate spot and press ENTER. Unfortunately the manual fails to mention that you may only move the cursor *forward* through the text. The implication of this statement is that if you inadvertently move the cursor *beyond* the place where you wish to mark the end of the block, you cannot move the cursor back up the text to the desired location. If you make this mistake you have no option but to abort the COPY command with ESC and start the whole procedure again!

Furthermore the COPY command seems to be designed on the assumption that you will only be marking small blocks and moving them short distances in the text. Suppose, for example, you have marked the beginning of the chapter, ideally you would like to move to the end of the chapter by means of the **cursor paragraph down** command or the GOTO command. Quill does not allow you to do this. The only cursor functions available to you while you are marking a block are:

● cursor left
● move cursor a word to the right
● cursor down

In other words, you would have to proceed line by line through the text using the cursor down key until you reach the end of the chapter. As you may imagine, this is a pretty slow business with a long chapter. If marking a large block is a tedious business then moving it a long distance is potentially even worse. For example, if you wish to move a paragraph from page 1 to page 20, you would once again have to proceed paragraph by paragraph through 19 pages! Of course this is just ridiculous. It would probably be faster to move directly to page 20 using the GOTO command and type the paragraph in again!

The reason why I have spent so much time on criticizing this command is that we have been promised further versions of Quill and QL owners should impress upon Sinclair that this is the command that needs to be improved as soon as possible.

The ERASE command

The **ERASE** command (**F3** and **E**) allows you to delete blocks of text. A block is marked in exactly the same way as in the COPY command. Once you have defined the block to be erased, you erase it by pressing ENTER. You are restricted to the same set of cursor commands as in the COPY command.

Chapter 6

ON-SCREEN FORMATTING

When you create a document you have to make a number of decisions concerning its layout and appearance:

The margins – how many characters to each line
The page length – the maximum number of lines on a page
The tab settings, etc. – the number and type of tab stops

Formatting commands

The instructions that control the appearance of a document are known as formatting commands. With most word processors, the formatting commands are only activated during the printing of a document. The great disadvantage of this approach is that the page format you see on the screen need not bear any relation to the layout of the printed document. In effect you have to guess what the document will look like when it is printed. Invariably you become immersed in an irritating cycle of inputting the formatting commands; printing a section of the document; evaluating the appearance; if it is unsatisfactory then changing formatting commands; printing a section of the document again; checking the layout; if it is unsatisfactory . . .

In contrast, Quill displays a document in the same format as it will eventually appear on paper. On-screen formatting, as this is called, enables you to judge the appearance of a document without wasting the time and paper required for numerous sample printouts. Quill's formatting commands take effect immediately, making it easy to experiment with different layouts.

Margins

Setting margins for a new document
To set the margins you press **F3** and **M**. The menu changes and you are offered the opportunity to alter the settings for the **Left, Indent** and **Right** margins. The default settings for the left and right margins are 1 and 80 respectively.

The third option – indent – probably requires some explanation. Whenever you press the ENTER key, Quill moves the cursor down to the next line but not necessarily to the *first* character position on the line. The cursor moves to the column specified by the 'indent' margin. The default setting for 'indent' is the 10th column. This is the reason why the cursor is positioned in the 10th column on the first line, when you first load Quill.

The procedure for setting all three margins is essentially the same. First you select the margin you wish to alter. Initially the 'left' margin option is highlighted in the menu. Highlighting is used to identify the margin that is going to be moved. If you don't wish to change the left margin, press the space bar and you will see the highlighting jump to 'indent'. Repeated pressing of the space bar causes the highlighting to cycle through the three options. So if you wanted to move the right margin you press the space bar until 'right' is highlighted. It is worth noting that you may type L, I or R to select the left, indent or right margin respectively.

Once you have selected the margin to be changed, you simply move the cursor to the column where you want the margin located. If you wish you may alter all the margin settings by selecting each margin in turn and moving the cursor to the appropriate columns. The margin settings you select at the beginning of a document will apply to all subsequent paragraphs unless you deliberately change them.

Altering existing margins
Suppose you wish to alter the left and right margin settings of the first paragraph of Exercise 1 from 1 and 54 to 5 and 50 respectively. Move the cursor to any line in the first paragraph and press F3 and M. The cursor jumps directly to the top left-hand corner of the paragraph. This happens for two reasons:

1   The margin command operates on complete paragraphs.
2   The command defaults to the left margin so Quill positions the cursor conveniently on the left side of the screen. If you select the right margin, the cursor moves to the top right-hand corner of the paragraph.

To set the left margin, move the cursor to column 5 (the

ruler line tells you the current position of the cursor). As the cursor moves along the line, it will drag the left margin with it. You can set the right margin in a similar way. Don't forget that if you are making drastic changes to a margin setting, then you can move the cursor a word at a time as well as a character at a time.

You will notice that altering the margin for the first paragraph has not affected the margins in the second paragraph. This should not surprise you since the margin commands act on individual paragraphs, not whole documents. Suppose you had another twenty paragraphs in Exercise 1 that you wanted to reformat to match the margin settings of the first paragraph. You could of course repeat the procedure described above for all twenty paragraphs in turn. This would certainly achieve your objective but it would be an extremely slow and tedious business.

Fortunately there is a faster method that is based on the fact that a margin setting applies to the whole of a paragraph. Imagine you have two successive paragraphs in a document with differing margins. You would like the second paragraph to be in the same format as the preceding one. If you merge the two paragraphs by deleting the carriage return and line-feed at the end of the first paragraph, the margin settings of the first paragraph will be automatically applied to the portion of the text that was previously the other paragraph. If you now hit the ENTER key, the two paragraphs will be separated again, except this time they will both have the same margin settings.

Let us demonstrate this technique using the two paragraphs in Exercise 1. The first paragraph now has margin settings of 5 and 50, while the second has margin settings of 1 and 64. Move the cursor to the C in 'Correcting'. Delete the carriage return and line-feed at the end of the first paragraph by hitting CTRL ←. The two paragraphs will merge. Now press ENTER and the second paragraph is reformed with the same margin settings as the previous paragraph!

If you had a further twenty paragraphs to reformat, you could move swifly from paragraph to paragraph using SHIFT ↓ , changing the margins as you went along. This approach is not entirely satisfactory but it is the quickest way to reformat a whole document with new margins.

Sometimes you need to indent every line of a paragraph, for example when you wish to produce numbered lists or paragraphs. Many word processors make it extremely difficult or impossible to produce numbered paragraphs. Even if they handle them at all they invariably do so in an awkward and clumsy manner. Quill produces an elegant solution to this problem. The key to the problem is to place the 'indent' margin to the *left* of the left margin.

Indent	Left	Right
:	:	:
:	:	:
1	The cursor remains within the left and right margin until you press ENTER.	
2	The cursor then jumps to the 'indent' margin. You may then type in the number of the paragraph or any other text providing it does not extend beyond the 'left' margin. Please note that you must not include a space in the text typed at the 'indent' margin because a space causes Quill to place all subsequent text within the normal margins.	

Justification

Quill treats the text you type in as a continuous stream of words and spaces. It fills up each line by extracting as many words as possible from this stream with the proviso that no word extends beyond the right margin. Normally the extracted words and spaces do not fill exactly the width of the line specified by your margins. Because Quill never splits a word in order to fit it on a line, an area of 'white space' is left at the end of each line giving the right-hand edge of text an uneven or 'ragged' appearance. If Quill leaves this white space at the end of the lines it is known as **left-justification**. If Quill removes the white space it is known as **right-justification**.

Left-justification
A typewriter produces left-justified text: the first character of each line begins at the left margin and the right margin has a ragged appearance.

> The text at the left margin in this
> paragraph forms a straight line while the   RAGGED
> text at the right-hand side of the page has   RIGHT
> a ragged appearance. This is the typical   MARGIN
> format of a page produced by a typewriter
> or by a cheap word processor which is
> incapable of producing right-justified
> text.

Right-justification
In contrast to a typewriter, Quill is capable of right-justifying text. When Quill right-justifies a line it removes all the spaces from the right end of the line – the white space – and distributes them as evenly as possible between the words on the line. As a result, the last word on each line ends at the right margin and the left and right edges of the text form straight lines.

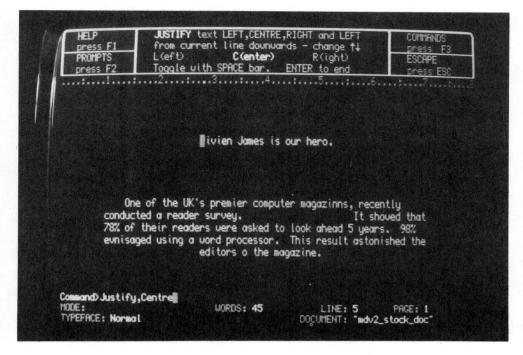

Figure 6.1   Justification using Quill

Right-justified text is one of the most prized features in a word-processing package. I have many reservations about the use of justified text which I have outlined in a later chapter on improving the appearance and readability of your documents.

STRAIGHT
RIGHT
MARGIN

Centre-justification
The term centre-justification normally refers to a method of formatting text where the inter-word spacing is equal in both directions from the centre of a line. Centre-justification is chiefly used for centering headings and titles in a text.

THIS IS A CENTRED TITLE
A SMALLER TITLE
A TINY TITLE
A TITLE
TITLE

The **JUSTIFY** command allows you to select the particular justification you want in your document. When you press **F3** and **J** you are offered three options: **Left**, **Centre** and **Right** justification. When you first load Quill it defaults to right-justified text and the JUSTIFY command is consistent in that it too defaults to right-justification.

You may select any of the options by moving the highlighting to the appropriate word in the menu and pressing ENTER. The justification command operates on a paragraph by paragraph basis. If you wish to change the justification of an existing paragraph, you simply move the cursor into the paragraph and then issue the appropriate justify command. It is surprisingly easy to reformat a large number of existing paragraphs by this method.

Tabulation

One of the most impressive aspects of Quill is its **TABS** command. Although almost all word processors let you set and clear tab stops, very few provide such a large variety of tabs or give you such complete control over where they are set. Quill imposes just one restriction on your use of tabs: only sixteen tab stops are allowed in one line. However, this is more than ample for most word-processing applications.

The TABULATE key on the QL operates in a similar way to the tab key on a typewriter. Pressing the TABULATE key moves the cursor to the nearest tab stop on the right. The tab stops are initially set at every tenth column, i.e. at the numbered positions on the ruler. You use the TABS command on the first command menu to set the type of tab and its position.

The four tab types
Quill provides four different types of tab stop: **left, right, centre** and **decimal**.

The **left** tab is the kind of tab stop you are familiar with on a typewriter. The *first* character of the words or numbers in a column are aligned.

> Left Tab
> 62.45
> 100
> Text typed at a left tab.

The **right** tab stop is unique to word processors. When you start typing at a right tab stop, the cursor remains stationary and the text typed in is shunted to the left. As a result the *last* character of the words or numbers in a column are aligned.

> Right tab
> 62.45
> 100
> Text typed at a right tab

The **centre** tab is useful for centering headings and titles. The text typed at a centre tab stop is adjusted so that the characters are centred about the tab stop. In effect it

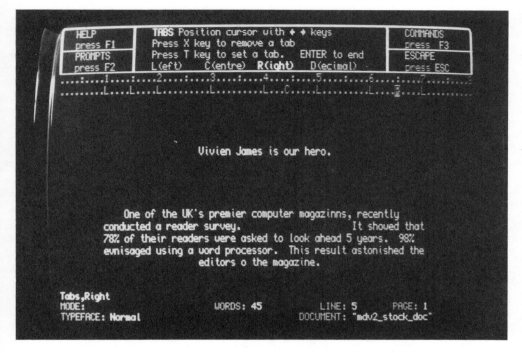

Figure 6.2   Using tabs with Quill

operates as a centre text command.

Centre tab
62.45
100
Text typed at a centre tab

Decimal tabs solve the perennial problem of aligning a column of decimal numbers on the decimal points. A decimal number typed at a tab stop is adjusted so that the decimal point is positioned at the tab stop. A decimal tab stop acts as a right tab stop for integers or ordinary text.

Decimal tab
62.45
5678.99
345.789
100
4345
Text typed at a decimal tab

Using the TABS command

Pressing the **F3** and **T** activates the TABS command. The menu displays the four options available and a second ruler line appears below the normal ruler. This tabs ruler shows the position and type of each tab stop in the current paragraph, for example, the initial tabs ruler with a left tab stop at every tenth character appears thus:

——— L ———L———L ——— L ——— L———

A tabs ruler showing a variety of tab stops:

–L——— L ——— R——— L——— C——— D ———

The type of each tab stop is marked in the tabs ruler by the appropriate letters: 'L' – left, 'R' – right, 'C' – centre, 'D' – decimal. Also a second cursor appears at the beginning of the tabs ruler. The cursor left and cursor right keys move this cursor backwards and forwards along the ruler.

The procedure for setting and clearing tabs is very straightforward and a pleasure to use.

- Move the cursor to the part of the text where you wish the tabs to take effect.
- Press F3 and T.
- Move the highlighting to the type of tab you want and press the appropriate letter (L,R,C, or D).
- Move the tabs cursor along the ruler to the place where you wish to set the tab and then press ENTER.
- Further tabs may be set in exactly the same way.

It really could not be easier!

Deleting a tab stop

Deleting a tab stop is as easy as setting one. Move the tabs cursor to the tab stop you wish to delete and press X. The tab stop is deleted instantly. A minor quibble is that there is no single command to delete all existing tab stops.

The tab stops you set will remain in effect until you explicitly change them.

A word of warning is required about trying to alter the existing tab stops in a paragraph. When you issue the TABS command, the tabs ruler displays the tab settings that were used to create that paragraph. If you alter the tab settings for that paragraph it can have an unpredictable affect on the format of the text.

The TABS command may be used to alter the layout of a set of tables. Suppose for example you have created a couple of tables using a particular set of tab settings, and then you decide that you wish to adjust the position of the tables on the page. For example:

——————L ———L ———————————————

450	156
750	345
67	987
123	788

To change the location of these tables you simply change the tab settings for this part of the text and the tables are moved automatically to the new tab settings. For example:

————————L————————	————L————————
450	156
750	345
67	987
123	788

Page breaks

Quill initially sets the number of lines to a page at 66. If you wish to alter this value you must use the DESIGN command which I will discuss later.

Sometimes you may wish to start a new page before you have completely filled the page you are on. You may wish to do this for all sorts of good reasons: to start a new chapter, to avoid splitting a table across two pages, to ensure that a list of instructions are kept together, etc. Quill allows you to insert a **page break** at any point in a text. If you insert a page break, then all subsequent text will be printed on the next page.

The page break command is on the second command menu, so you need to press **F3** and **OP**. Place the cursor at the place in the text where you want to insert the page break and then hit ENTER. Quill returns to the main menu and the screen now displays the page break line.

———————————————————— end of page 10————

Deleting a page break
To delete a page break which you have inserted, place the cursor on the page break line and then press CTRL and →.

Hyphenation

Right justification eliminates 'white space' at the end of lines by distributing the spaces as evenly as possible between the words. Sometimes this results in unusually large gaps between the words on a line. Very wide spacing between words is most likely to occur if a line includes a number of very long words. One technique for producing more regular spacing between words is to **hyphenate** words that would otherwise be moved down to the next line by Quill's word wrap facility. Here is an example to demonstrate how an appropriately placed hyphen improves the appearance of a section of text.

Without hyphen

Text which has a very uneven spacing between the words due to wordwrapping is extremely difficult to comprehend and assimilate. A wide inter-word spacing constitutes a form of unintended punctuation which sometimes may interrupt the natural pattern of eye movements.

With hyphen

Text which has a very uneven spacing between the words due to wordwrapping is extremely difficult to comprehend and assimilate. A wide inter-word spacing constitutes a form of unin-tended punctuation which sometimes may inter-rupt the natural pattern of eye movements.

Notice how a single hyphen significantly reduces the word spacing in the last three lines of the paragraph. However a problem may arise if we subsequently rewrite the text. The hyphens in 'unintended' and 'interrupt' have been inserted on the assumption that the words fall at the end of a line. Any change to the passage may result in these words being moved away from the end of the line. It would then be necessary to delete the hyphens. It would be very convenient if we could insert hyphens that would be automatically deleted by Quill in the event of them being moved from the end of lines. In other words we want two kinds of hyphens in our text:

1   Hyphens that we wish to be preserved regardless of how the text is reformatted. These **hard** hyphens are the kind you insert in words that are always hyphenated, e.g. self-determination, high-class, hunky-dory, etc.
2   Hyphens that are inserted in words that fall at the end of lines. However should a subsequent change to the text lead to a situation where a hyphenated word no longer falls at the end of a line, then Quill should automatically remove the hyphen from the word. We might call these **soft** hyphens to contrast them with the permanent kind described above.

A *hard* hyphen is inserted by using the hyphen key on the keyboard.

A *soft* hyphen is inserted with the **HYPHENATE** command which is on the second command menu. Press **F3** and **OH** and the menu tells you to move the cursor to the character *following* the position where you wish to insert the hyphen. To insert the hyphen you press ENTER.

Chapter 7

SPECIAL PRINTING AND DISPLAY COMMANDS

Quill is able to underline text, produce **bold** text and generate super^{scripts} and sub$_{scripts}$. Furthermore, it is possible to use more than one of these features at the same time. For example you may create bold underlined text, bold superscripts or even underlined subscripts should should the urge come upon you. However, it is important to realise that you will not be able to reproduce these features in your documents unless your printer supports them as well. Fortunately, this particular set of special print characteristics are becoming standard on most decent printers, especially dot-matrix printers. You may discover that some printers will not allow you to use more than one feature at a time.

The TYPEFACE command

To call the TYPEFACE command simply press **F4**. The menu displays five options, the four I have referred to above and a fifth option called **painting** which I shall discuss in a moment. Because the words 'superscript' and 'subscript' both begin with the same letter ('s'), Quill has been forced to adopt the rather artifical terms 'high' and 'low', to refer to 'superscript' and 'subscript' respectively.

To select a typeface you press the appropriate letter, B, L, H, or U. All text you subsequently type will be entered in the chosen typeface. When you wish to change to another typeface or to revert back to normal text, you must switch off the current typeface explicitly. A typeface is switched on and off with the same command, i.e. you **toggle** the typefaces on and off. So you would use **F4** and **U** to switch underlining on and off.

To use two typefaces at the same time, you must call the TYPEFACE command twice. Imagine you wish to have bold, underlined text. The sequence of commands is:

- F4 B selects bold text.
- F4 U selects underlined text.

The status area now displays TYPEFACE:BOLD,UNDERLINE. As you might expect, you would need to repeat this sequence of commands if you wanted to revert to normal text.

In effect, Quill allows you to mark blocks of text with a particular typeface or combination of typefaces. Consequently if you insert some additional text *within* an existing block of text, it is automatically assigned the typefaces attached to that section of text. So text inserted in a block of bold text is automatically entered as bold text. In other words you would not need to select bold text before you made the insertion.

However suppose you wish to insert a passage of underlined, normal text within a block of bold text. Essentially your objective is to replace a single block of bold text with three successive blocks of bold text, normal underlined text and bold text.

I will insert a passage of underlined normal text in this block of bold text. The procedure for doing this is relatively straightforward but you need to make sure that you explicitly switch off bold text before making the insertion.

I will insert a passage of underlined normal text in this block of bold text. <u>This is the additional underlined text.</u> **The procedure for doing this is relatively straightforward but you need to make sure that you explicitly switch off bold text before making the insertion.**

The procedure to insert this underlined text is as follows:

1 Move the cursor to where you wish to make the insertion.
2 Switch off bold text with **F4 B**.
3 Switch on underlined text with **F4 U**.
4 Type in the additional text.
5 Switch off underlined text with **F4 U**.

Painting

The paint option in the TYPEFACE command allows you to remove or change the typeface that you have attached to a block of text. Suppose you wish to alter a section of normal text to bold text. You move the cursor to the beginning of the section and then you select the paint option with **F4** and **P**. The menu asks you to select the typeface or typefaces you

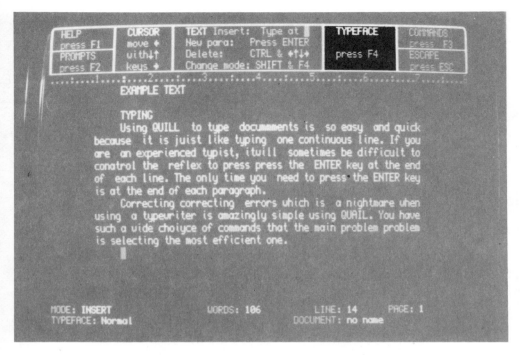

Figure 7.1   The typeface command

wish to apply. In this case you would press B for bold text. As you move the cursor *forward* through the text you want to change, you will see it transformed into bold text. When you reach the end of the section you wish to change, you press ESC and you are returned to the main menu.

The paint option suffers from the same problem as all the other Quill commands that manipulate blocks of text. The cursor may only be moved forward through the text. There is no means of retracing your steps if you inadvertently go beyond the point you intended. To paint a large block of text takes a very long time because you cannot use any of the 'long-distance' cursor commands like GOTO or paragraph down.

The restriction on the cursor commands in the paint option is particularly serious if you are using a dot-matrix printer, because to approximate to near-letter-quality output on a dot-matrix printer you will need to print the whole document in bold text. A dot-matrix printer will print a document in bold text very much more slowly than it will a document in normal text. A common practice is to bash out draft copies of manuscripts as quickly as possible in normal text and only add bold text to the final, completed document. However to paint a whole document in bold text after it has been created using normal text is an extremely long and tedious business. It is the proverbial 'heads you lose, tails you lose' situation. If you create the document using bold text then every draft will take an inordinately long time to print. If you create the document using normal text you then have the chore of painting the whole document in bold before the final printing.

Headers   A header is a line of text that is printed at the top of each page. For example, you may wish to head every page with the title of the document or the name of the chapter. Sometimes it is necessary to remind the reader of the status of a document so you might use a header such as 'Confidential' or 'Provisional'. The **HEADER** command allows you to specify a line of text including a page number if desired. Once you have specified the header, Quill will automatically add the header to each printed page. The header is not however shown on the screen.

To insert a header in your text you press **F3** and **H**. First you are asked to specify where the header is to be printed on the line. It may be placed at the *left* margin, in the *centre* or at the *right* margin. A fourth option None is used to switch off an existing header. After you have positioned the header you are asked to type in the appropriate text. You are restricted to one line of text for your header and a page number may be included *anywhere* within the header.

Page numbers
Quill provides three different formats for the page number:

Arabic numerals: e.g. 1,2,3,4, . . .
Roman numerals: e.g. I,II,III,IV, . . .
Alphabetic: e.g. A,B,C,D, . . .

Each format has its own unique code:

nnn or NNN	signifies	Arabic numerals
rrr or RRR	signifies	Roman numerals
aaa or AAA	signifies	Alphabetic

Quill scans the header looking for these codes and if it finds one of them it automatically substitutes the corresponding type of page number.

Example: a header on page 4

Header text:	INTRODUCTION TO WORD PROCESSING nnn
Printed as:	INTRODUCTION TO WORD PROCESSING page 4
Header text:	RRR Chapter 1: The Hardware
Printed as:	page IV Chapter 1: The Hardware

Header text: Word Processing   aaa   Chapter 1: The
Printed as: Hardware
                Word Processing   page D   Chapter 1: The
                Hardware

Before you exit from the header command you must specify:

● The number of lines to be left blank between the header and the main text (the header margin). You are allowed a maximum of 9 lines between the header and the main text. This is more than adequate for most purposes.

● Whether you wish to have the header printed in **bold** or normal text. The default is bold text.

Footers
A footer is a line of text that will be printed as the *last* line of text on a page. The **FOOTER** command, **F3** and **F**, works in broadly the same way as the HEADER command. The only difference is that Quill automatically provides a page number as footer unless you specify otherwise. This default footer is a centred, Arabic numeral.

The DESIGN command

There are a number of formatting commands that are not listed as separate commands on the command menus. Line spacing, page length, top and bottom margins, display width, and a number of other features are all controlled by the **DESIGN** command.

When you select the DESIGN command by pressing **F3** and **D**, the screen displays the list of formatting features shown in Figure 7.2. These features are listed in alphabetical order and each one starts with a different letter of the alphabet. The default values for each option are displayed on the right of the screen.

Bottom margin (type No and ENT)	3
Display width 80, 64, 40, (8,6,4)	64
Gaps between the lines (0,1,2)	0
Page size (type No and ENT)	6
Start page number (type No and ENT)	1
Type colour	GRN
Upper margin (type No and ENT)	6

The procedure for altering these values is essentially the same for each option. If, for example, you wish to alter the number of lines to a page, press P – the first letter of the option. The option you have selected is highlighted and you are prompted to enter a new value for the option.

While you are in the DESIGN command you may change one or all the values for the options. What should you do if

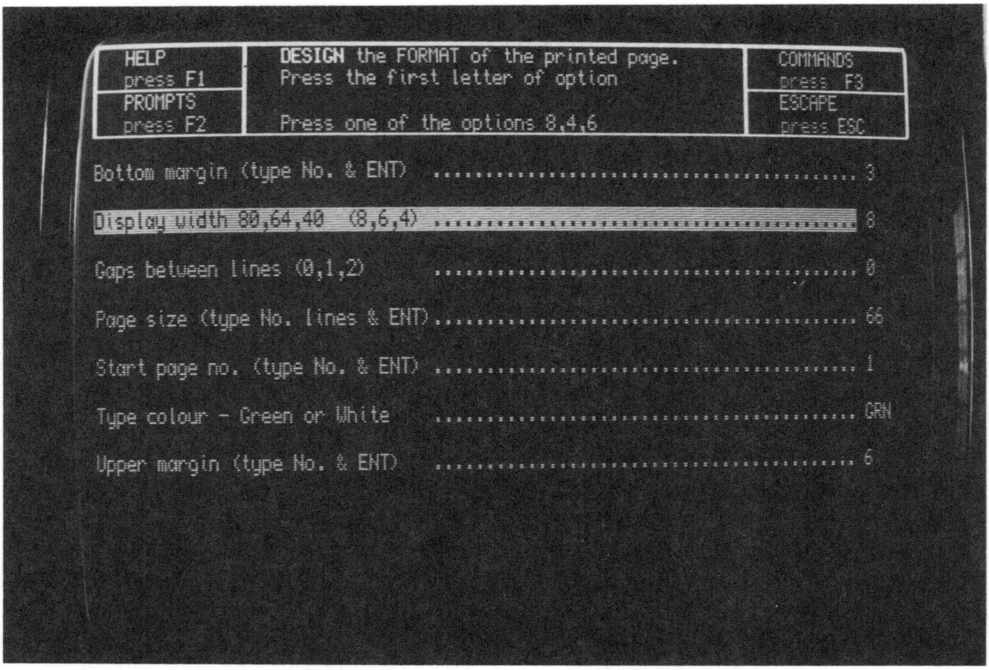

Figure 7.2   The Quill screen showing options in DESIGN command

you select an option by mistake? You must enter the
original value again. If you just hit ENTER the value will be
zeroed. What you definitely must not do is hit ESC. If you
press ESC, you not only exit from the DESIGN command
but also you will lose any alterations you made while you
were in the DESIGN command. The ESC is a signal to Quill
to abort the command and to ignore the changes you made.
You must exit from the DESIGN command by pressing
ENTER. Let us make sure you understand the difference
between ESC and ENTER in this context:

ENTER   Save all the changes and exit to the main menu
ESC   Ignore all the changes and return to the main
              menu

The options in the DESIGN command may be divided into
two categories: formatting commands which control the
layout of the printed document and formatting commands
which determine how text is displayed on the screen. I shall
first discuss the options which relate to the printed page, i.e.

Upper margin
Bottom margin
Gaps between the lines
Page size
Start page number

Upper margin
The upper margin is the number of lines between the top of the page and the first line of text. The default is 6 lines. If you wish to have a header on the first line of the page you should set the upper margin to 0.

You will have to experiment with the size of the upper margin. Normally it is not necessary to specify an upper margin when you are using single sheets of paper in your printer. Often the feed mechanism on a printer does not allow you to align the top of the paper with the printhead. In effect, the mechanics of using single sheets on a printer lead to an upper margin whether you like it or not. In fact the printhead may be positioned as much as four lines down from the top of a sheet. Suppose you wanted an upper margin of 8 lines. If you use the DESIGN command to change the value of the upper margin to 8, it will result in an *actual* upper margin of 12 lines on the printed sheet. The additional four lines arise from the starting position of the paper within the printer.

The same problem does not arise with fanfold paper. If you are willing to waste the top sheet of paper, you can align the printhead with the beginning of the second sheet, i.e. along the perforations joining the first and second sheet. Any margin you then specify with the DESIGN command will be accurate.

Bottom margin
The bottom margin is the number of blank lines from the last line of text to the bottom of the page. Normally the last line of text is the footer. The default is 3 lines.

Gaps between the lines
This option specifies the number of blank lines to be inserted between each line of text. You are provided with three alternatives:

    0: Single spacing   i.e. no blank lines inserted
    1: Double spacing   i.e. one blank line inserted
    2: Triple spacing   i.e. two blank lines inserted

The default is single spacing. Please note that this command does not affect the display of text on the screen. The text on the screen is always displayed as single-spaced.

Page size
The page size specifies the maximum number of lines to be included on a page. It defaults to 66 lines which is perhaps a shade too few for A4 paper. Word processors that originate from the USA often default to 66 lines as well, but American A4 paper is slightly smaller than our A4 paper. I find that 70 lines per page is about right. The important

point is that 66 lines per page is not some international standard that you must abide by. The page size you choose will depend on a number of factors including the size of paper and the inter-line spacing on your printer. A typical page might be comprised as follows:

Upper margin: 2
Header line: 1
Header margin: 3
Main text: 50   (single spacing)
Footer margin: 4
Footer line: 1
Bottom margin: 5
Total   66 lines

If you decide to print a document with this layout using double spacing then you would only have 25 lines of main text on each page.

Sometimes you may not want a document to be split into pages, for example when you are typing in assembly language programs. You can stop Quill dividing the text into pages by setting the page size to zero.

Start page number
Quill assumes you will wish to start each new file on page 1. The page number is then incremented by 1 on each successive page. If you split a large document over a number of files, then you will need to use this option to continue the pagination from one file to another.

Display options

The remaining two options in the DESIGN command control the display of text on the screen. They do not influence the layout of the printed document. They are:

Display width
Type colour

Display width
Quill displays lines of 64 characters on a television and lines of 80 characters on a monitor. This option allows you to alter the number of characters to 40, 64 or 80 (4,6,8). There is no point in trying to display 80 characters per line on a television, the characters would be so indistinct as to be unreadable. On the other hand, if you are using a poor-quality television you may find lines of 40 characters to be the optimum display width.

Type colour
When you first load Quill, normal text is displayed in green

and bold text is displayed in white. The type colour option enables you to reverse this and display normal text in white and bold text in green.

The VIEW command

One of Quill's great strengths is its ability to display a document on the screen in the same format as the printed document. However, if you create a document with very long line-lengths then the text at the end of the lines disappears off the right-hand side of the screen. It becomes extremely difficult to evaluate the layout of a document when you can only see a portion of it at any one time.

The **VIEW** command allows you to see the layout of your document. When you press **F3** and **OV**, the screen undergoes a remarkable transformation: each text character is replaced by a small block but the punctuation characters are displayed in their normal form. So although you will not be able to read the text you will be able to see its general layout.

The VIEW command switches this special format on and off.

In a later chapter I will discuss how to use these formatting commands to improve the layout of your documents.

Chapter 8

PRINTING YOUR DOCUMENTS

Installing a
printer

Although word processors are increasingly being used to
generate text to be transferred directly to other computers,
their primary function is still to produce printed
documents. Linking a word processor to a printer so that
they work smoothly together is often the biggest headache
you face when you first venture into word processing. The
procedure for matching a word processor to a printer is
called *installing the printer.*

Any reasonable printer will be able to print in a variety of
print modes, i.e. produce bold text, underlined text, etc.
How does the printer know when to shift from one print
mode to another? The explanation is that Quill embeds
printer control codes in the document files it creates. When
the printer detects one of these control codes it responds by
changing to the print mode which corresponds to that
control code. For example, if you send ESC E to an FX-80
printer, it is a signal to the printer to print all subsequent
text in boldface. The FX-80 will continue to print in
boldface until it receives the control code that switches off
bold printing, i.e. ESC F.

The paragraph on the left below shows the text with the
embedded control codes. The paragraph on the right shows
the *effect* of having the control codes in the text. The control
codes are shown in boldface to distinguish them from text.

This is how the file
appears to the FX-80
printer. **ESCE**Bold text is
switched on and off with
the appropriate control
codes**ESCF**. Underlined
text **ESC-O**appears like
this**ESC-1**.

This is how the file
appears to the FX-80
printer. **Bold text is
switched on and off with
the appropriate control
codes.** Underlined text
appears like this.

Unfortunately there is no agreed standard for printer control codes and each printer has its own unique set of codes. If you send FX-80 control codes to a different model of printer, the control codes will almost certainly be misinterpreted and this is likely to produce some very undesirable results! It is vital, therefore, that Quill uses the set of control codes appropriate to your printer. Quill uses the control codes that it finds in a file called 'printer—dat' which is on the Quill cartridge. If you are not using an FX-80 you will need to insert the control codes for your printer into 'printer—dat'. A SuperBASIC program called **install—bas** has been provided to enable you to insert these codes into 'printer—dat'.

Also on the cartridge is a file called 'install—dat'. Over a period of time you may well use a number of printers with your QL. Each time you install a printer, the installation data is stored in 'install—dat'. 'Install—dat' is a file of records; each record contains, amongst other things, the control codes for a particular printer. The structure of each record is exactly the same as the structure of 'printer—dat'.

When you run the program 'install—bas', it first searches through 'install—dat' for the names of printers you have installed in the past. It lists the printers it finds and invites you to choose one of them. If you select one of these printers, 'install—bas' copies the record for that printer from 'install—dat' into 'printer—dat'.

The QL manual has a pretty comprehensive guide to installing printers, so there is little point in me repeating the information here. However there are a number of practical difficulties in installing a printer that need to be discussed. I will use the example of the FX-80 since this is the printer that is discussed in the QL manual.

Printer—dat for the FX-80

Driver name	:FX-80
Parity	:None
Baud rate	:9600
Lines/page	:66
Characters/line	:80
Continuous forms	:Yes
End-of-line code	:<CR>,<LF>
End-of-page code	:<FF>
Preamble code	:<ESC>,@,<ESC>,R,3
Postamble code	:None
Emphasize on	:<ESC>,E
Emphasize off	:<ESC>,F
Underline on	:<ESC>,−,1
Underline off	:<ESC>,−,0
Subscript on	:<ESC>,1

Subscript off	:<ESC>,T
Superscript on	:<ESC>,S,0
Superscript off	:<ESC>,T
Translate1	:£,
Translate2	:None

The FX-80 installation data listed above assumes that you are using continuous forms (fanfold paper) with your printer. If you decide to use single sheets of paper you are told in the manual to run 'install_bas' and set Continuous forms to No. Unfortunately life is not quite that simple.

The FX-80 has a facility for detecting when it has run out of paper. As the last sheet of paper passes through the printer it triggers a small pressure switch in the paper-feed mechanism causing a buzzer to sound and the printer immediately stops printing. The pressure switch is positioned in such a way that the printing stops about two-thirds of the way down the last sheet of paper. Consequently it is impossible to print a complete page of text if you are using single sheets of paper. It is possible to overcome this problem by switching off the paper-end detector. There are two methods for doing this:

1 Open up the machine with a screwdriver and flick the relevant switch.
2 Send down the control code **ESC 8** before you start printing.

Therefore with a printer like the FX-80, it is *not* sufficient to set the value of Continuous forms to No. You must also switch off the paper-end detector. I will now show you how to do this by a method which may be of value to you even if you do not own an FX-80 printer.

Unless you intend to always use single sheets of paper, it is not really advizable to permanently switch off the end-of-paper detector. The most convenient way to switch off the paper-end detector is to include the control code ESC 8 in Preamble in printer_dat. The control codes stored in Preamble are sent to the printer before it starts printing. Therefore it is possible to switch off the paper-end detector without resorting to the screwdriver! In effect I am suggesting that you install the FX-80 *twice* under two different names, e.g. FX-80C and FX-80S. FX-80C will contain the installation data for single sheets. The difference between the two sets of data is shown below.

	FX-80C	**FX-80S**
Continuous forms	:YES	:NO
Preamble code	:<ESC>,@,<ESC>,R,3	:<ESC>,@<ESC>,R,3,<ESC>,8

The really significant difference between the two sets of

data is the control code, ESC 8, which turns off the paper-end detector.

Now suppose you wish to use single sheets with your FX-80. First you run 'install_bas' using:

lrun MDV1_install_bas <ENTER>

The program offers you a list of printers including FX-80S and FX-80C. Since you wish to switch off the paper-end detector you need to select FX-80S. The data from FX-80S is copied into 'printer_dat'. You should now be able to use single sheets without any problems. The next time you wish to use fanfold paper, you repeat the above procedure but this time you select FX-80C.

Quill provides superscripts and subscripts as two of its four print modes. These are extremely valuable to technical authors and writers who are using a foreign language with lots of accents on the letters. However I am sure that many users of Quill will find little or no use for superscripts and subscripts. I think I last needed to use a subscript about five years ago! With only four print modes available, it is very frustrating to be provided with two modes that are so rarely used. It is particularly annoying when you have a printer which supports facilities that you frequently use but Quill does not allow you to include them in your documents. For example, when I am working with other word processors, I frequently make use of 'large' text and 'condensed' text. It would be very nice if we could find some way of adapting Quill to provide these print modes. Let us see how we might approach this problem.

Suppose you run 'install_bas' and install the FX-80 again, but this time you replace the control codes for superscripts and subscripts with the control codes for the print modes that you want, e.g. in my case the control codes for 'large' text and 'condensed' text.

An FX-80 installed for large and condensed text

Subscript on	:<ESC>,SI	Condensed on
Subscript off	:<DC2>	Condensed off
Superscript on	:<ESC>,W,1	Large on
Superscript off	:<ESC>,W,0	Large off

By inserting the control codes for large and condensed text in the slots for superscripts and subscripts, we will fool Quill into thinking it is generating superscripts and subscripts on the printer when it is actually producing large and condensed text!

If you run Quill and then select TYPEFACE, you will still be offered H(igh) and L(ow) as options. Furthermore if you create some text using these options, the display continues to show the text in superscript and subscript format. However, and this is the important point, when the document is printed all subscripts will be printed in condensed text and all superscripts will be printed in large text. I know this is not entirely satisfactory but it does achieve the objective of making available some of the print modes you really need. With a little ingenuity (and patience), you should be able to exploit most of the features of your printer by means of this method.

The PRINT command

The **PRINT** command is on the first command menu and is called by **F3** and **P**. A number of alternatives are available to you:

- You may print the document you are currently editing or any other document residing on Microdrive 2.
- You may print the *whole* of a document or a specified range of pages from the document, e.g. pages 4 to 8.
- Instead of printing the document on the printer, you may print the document to a file.

After you press F3 and P, the command line displays 'Print, current'. Quill is assuming that you probably wish to print the document you are currently working on. To print the current document, you press ENTER, otherwise you must enter the name of the file that you wish to print. After you have selected the document you wish to print, Quill suggests that you print the whole of the document and the command line now shows 'Print, current, whole'. Once again you press ENTER to accept Quill's suggestion that you print the complete document. The other alternative is to enter the first number of the range of pages you wish to print, e.g. 4. In this case the command line now displays 'Print, current, from page 4 to end'. Quill now expects you to complete the range of pages to be printed. If you wish to print from page 4 to the end of the document, you press ENTER, otherwise you must enter a page number e.g. 8. It is at this stage that you have to decide whether to send the document to the printer or to print it to a file on the Microdrive. Pressing ENTER causes the document to be printed on the printer. If you enter a filename, then Quill stores the document as a print-file on the Microdrive, e.g. 'Print, current, from page 2 to 4 print__doc' stores the document you are currently editing as a file called 'print__ doc' on the Microdrive.

Examples
These are the keystrokes required to print the following:

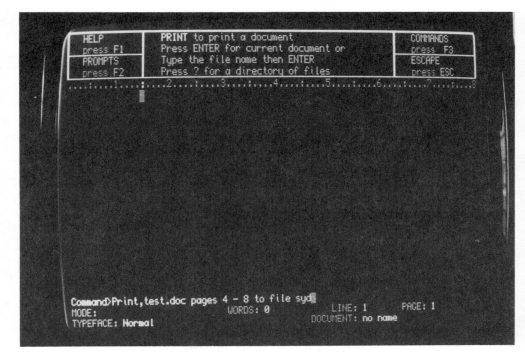

Figure 8.1   The Quill screen showing the PRINT option

Figure 8.2   Printing a document

```
PRINT
=====

To print all or part of a document.

In response to the first prompt press ENTER to print the
document being edited (or written); alternatively type in a
file name, followed by ENTER.

Then to print the whole document press ENTER; otherwise specify
start page number and press ENTER to print to the end of the
document or specify end page number.

Finally press ENTER to send the output to printer; alternatively

type in a file name so that result goes to a file (or net).

Additional information :-

Directories     Files

?
```

1   The whole of the current document:

     F3 P <ENTER><ENTER><ENTER>

2   The whole of a document called 'exercise_doc':

     F3 P exercise <ENTER><ENTER><ENTER>

3   Pages 4 to 8 of 'exercise_doc':

     F3 P exercise <ENTER>4<ENTER>8<ENTER><ENTER>

4   The whole of 'exercise_doc' to a new file called 'test_doc':

     F3 P exercise <ENTER><ENTER>test<ENTER><ENTER>

5   Pages 4 to 8 of 'exercise_doc' to a new file called 'test_doc':

     F3 P exercise <ENTER>4<ENTER<8<ENTER> test<ENTER><ENTER>

The manual states that pressing ESC will cause the printer to cease printing a document. However with my version of Quill, pressing ESC not only stops the printer but it also causes Quill to 'hang-up'. This means that you have no choice but to reset the QL and reload Quill. Quill will also 'hang-up' in the following circumstances:

1   The printer is not connected.
2   The printer is not switched on.
3   The printer malfunctions during the printing of a document.

If Quill hangs-up you will lose the document you are working on. I would recommend you adopt the habit of *always* saving a document before you attempt to print it. This will ensure that you never lose your hard work in the event of Quill crashing!

Chapter 9

HANDLING YOUR FILES

Quill has an extensive array of file-handling commands which are the mark of a powerful word processor. These commands correspond to normal office procedures for creating, revising and storing printed documents:

Printed documents	Quill
Labelling a document	NAME a file
Reviewing a document	LOAD a file
Store a document for later use	SAVE a file
Discard a document	DELETE or ZAP a file
Duplicate or photocopy a document	BACKUP copies of a file
Update a document with information from other documents	IMPORT or MERGE files

Naming files   A filename consists of three parts:

A Microdrive specifier	e.g. MDV2
A name (maximum length 8 characters)	e.g. accounts
A 3-character code called the extension	e.g. doc

The three parts of the filename *must* be linked with the underscore character ('_'). For example:

   MDV2_accounts_doc

If you do not specify the Microdrive when referring to a file then Quill assumes the file is on Microdrive 2.
   Quill will allocate the extension 'doc' to all documents unless you specify a different extension. Suppose you have just entered a new document and you wish to give it the

name 'accounts_doc'. When Quill prompts you for the filename, you enter 'accounts'. The file is then stored on the cartridge as 'accounts_doc'. If you do not wish the file to be stored on Microdrive 2, then you must include a Microdrive in the filename, e.g. 'MDV1_accounts'.

Examples of invalid filenames

MDV1:accounts_doc	The underscore has been replaced with a ':'
MDV2_information_doc	'information' is more than 8 characters
MDV3_members_list	The extension is more than 3 characters

The LOAD command

When you wish to look at an existing file you use the **LOAD** command which is called by **F3** and **L**. The command line displays LOAD, and you are prompted to enter the name of the file. If you cannot remember or are unaware of the exact name of the file then you may press '?' and Quill will display a list of all the files on Microdrive 2. If you are currently editing a document and you decide to load another file instead, then you must be careful because the LOAD command deletes the file you are working on and replaces it with the new file. If you wish to keep a copy of the file you are working on then you must save it before issuing the LOAD command.

The SAVE command

To keep permanent copies of the documents you create you must store them on a cartridge. The **SAVE** command, **F3** and **S**, stores a document on a cartridge under a filename of your own choice. When you ask Quill to save a document it prompts you to enter a filename. If it is a *new* document, i.e. one that has not previously been saved, then the command line displays SAVE, and the menu asks you to assign a filename to the document. Typing a filename followed by ENTER causes Quill to save the document. After the document has been successfully saved, you are offered two options:

1 Press ENTER to continue editing the document you have just saved.
2 Press *any other key* to start work on a different document. You may if you wish insert a new data cartridge in Microdrive 2 at this moment, in which case you should insert the cartridge *before* pressing a key.

When you load a file, Quill does not erase the file from the cartridge. It makes a copy of the file and transfers it into the

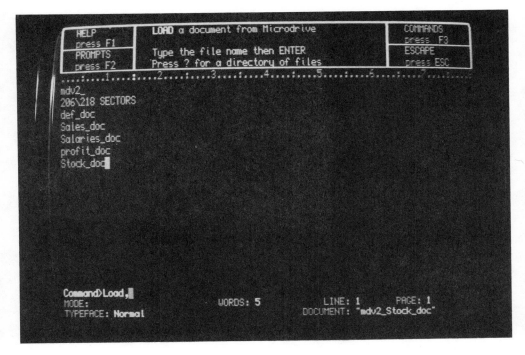

Figure 9.1   Screen showing directory of files

QL's memory. The original file on the cartridge remains
unchanged. Imagine you have loaded a file called
'accounts—doc', made some changes to it and now you
wish to save the updated version of the file. When you press
F3 and S, the command line shows 'Save, accounts'. Quill is
assuming that you will want to save the document under its
current name so it inserts the current filename in the
command line. You now have two options:

1 Press ENTER to accept Quill's suggestion that you save
   the document under its current name.
2 Type in a new filename. Quill will save the file under
   this new filename. Notice that this new filename now
   appears alongside Document in the status area. In effect
   you have *renamed* the document you are editing by
   saving it under a new name.

Before Quill saves a file it searches the directory of files on
the cartridge to make sure that a file of the same name does
not exist already. Quill will not overwrite an existing file
unless you confirm that this is what you want. So if you
accept Quill's suggestion that you save a file under its
current name, you are asked to confirm that you want this
new version of the file to replace the old version. Pressing Y
causes Quill to overwrite the old file. Pressing ESC aborts
the SAVE command.

When you are are creating a new document or revizing an existing one, you must adopt the habit of saving the document at regular intervals. The text stored in memory is much more vulnerable to loss than a document stored on a cartridge. I suggest you use the word count in the status area as a reminder of when to save a document. Every time I add 250 words to a document I save it. With this system, if something goes wrong, I never lose more than about half-a-page of text.

The FILES command

A number of file-handling commands do not appear on the menu under their individual names. The **FILES** command on the second command menu is in fact four distinct commands:

1　BACKUP　　option B
2　DELETE　　option D
3　FORMAT　　option F
4　IMPORT　　option I

The FILES command is **F3 OF**.

BACKUP
It is only prudent to make more than one copy of valuable documents. You could use the SAVE command to make a copy of a document but this has the disadvantage that the original and the copy would both be on the same cartridge. It is more sensible to store the copy on another cartridge. The BACKUP command is used to copy files from Microdrive 2 to Microdrive 1. This statement should surprise you. Normally it is not possible to remove the cartridge containing Quill from Microdrive 1: the program crashes. However the BACKUP command allows you to temporarily replace the Quill cartridge with a data cartridge. The command assumes that the file to be copied is on Microdrive 2 and that you want it copied to the cartridge in Microdrive 1.

You select the BACKUP option by pressing B. The command line displays 'Backup', and the menu prompts you to enter the name of the file to be copied, e.g. accounts_doc. The command line now shows 'Backup accounts to'. You then have to wait a few moments before you can remove the Quill cartridge. Quill informs you when it is safe to proceed. It is normal to use the same name for the backup copy as for the original. If you want to use a different name for the backup copy then you must type in a new filename, e.g. account_dat. The command line shows 'Backup, accounts to account_dat'. When Quill has finished making the backup copy, it reminds you to replace the Quill cartridge in Microdrive 1.

You should adopt the habit of *always* making backup copies of your important software and data. A systematic approach to protecting your software will cost you extra money in terms of cartridges but you will never regret the investment. Newcomers to computing invariably ignore this advice. Apparently they need the bitter experience of losing important documents before they take this advice seriously. Learn from the mistakes of others and use BACKUP on every important file.

DELETE
The **DELETE** option erases a file from a cartridge. You must remember that this is an irreversible command: once a document has been deleted it can never be recovered. Always think twice before using this command!

FORMAT
A new cartridge has to be formatted before it can be used on the QL. Trying to save data onto a cartridge that has not been formatted is a recipe for disaster. The Quill **FORMAT** command assumes that the blank cartridge is in Microdrive 1. Please note that Psion specifically state that you must *never* insert an unformatted cartridge in Microdrive 2.

IMPORT
The **IMPORT** option is very similar to the **MERGE** command on the second command menu. It will be more helpful if I discuss them together.

The MERGE command is used to merge two Quill documents. The IMPORT option of the FILES command is used to insert a file produced by one of the other Psion packages (Easel, Abacus and Archive) into a Quill document.

The MERGE command

Cut and paste is the common term for the word-processing commands that allow a section of text to be copied or moved *within* a document. The COPY command, if you remember, allows you to move or copy a block of text. A logical extension to this copy facility would be a command that allowed you to move text from one document to another. The MERGE command and the IMPORT option of the FILES command allow you to copy a file from a cartridge and insert it into the document you are currently editing.

The procedure for merging two documents is as follows:

● Move the cursor to the position where you want the file inserted.

● Issue the MERGE command with **F3** and **OM**.

● Type in the name of the file you want inserted. If this file is on another cartridge then you may insert that cartridge in Microdrive 1. You will then see the file inserted at the current position of the cursor.

● Press ESC to return to the main menu.

The QUIT command

When you wish to stop using Quill you use the **QUIT** command on the first command menu. After you have pressed **F3** and **Q**, the command line displays 'quit'. You are then offered three options:

1   Pressing ENTER saves the document you are currently working on. You may save it under its current name or under a different name if you wish.
2   Press A if you do not want the file saved. If the file has not previously been saved then it is irretrievably lost. Remember that abandoning the current version of a file does not mean that the previous version is erased from the cartridge. All you are doing is not saving the changes you have made in the current editing session.
3   Pressing ESC aborts the command.

The ZAP command

The **ZAP** command, **F3** and **OZ**, deletes the document you are currently working on. If you have not previously saved the text then it will be irretrievably lost. Sometimes you make so many mistakes in a file that it is easier to start again than try to make the corrections, in which case you simply 'zap' the file and start again.

Chapter 10

BEYOND QUILL

In some respects Quill is a state-of-the-art word processor. It is very user-friendly with a comprehensive set of menus and on-line help files. The on-screen formatting is comparable with the best word processors currently on the market. However, in other respects it does not measure up to what is now expected of a full-fledged, business word processor. In this chapter, I shall outline some of the features that are available in other, albeit more expensive, word processors. Hopefully many of these facilities will be incorporated in future versions of Quill.

Screen splitting

The most exciting development in word processing is the ability to split the screen into several **windows**. A window is the jargon for a section of the screen which acts like a miniature version of the full screen. The window technique allows you to edit one document while referring to another document. For example a word processor called Multi-tool Word lets you work with up to eight different documents on the screen at the same time! It is not difficult to imagine how useful such a facility must be when you are assembling a document from several others or you are shuffling text from one place to another in the same document. Think how convenient it would be if you could have all the drafts of a document on the screen at the same time. You would be able to take the best sections from each draft and literally drag them, on screen, into one final document. Windowing removes much of the drudgery from revizing and editing draft documents.

The QL's multitasking operating system is perfect for software designers who wish to incorporate a window facility into their programs.

Form letters and mailing lists

The most glaring omission from Quill is the facility to produce 'personalized' **form** letters. The letter boxes of the nation are stuffed with personalized letters from insurance companies, book clubs and all the other businesses who have acquired a word processor. A form letter is a letter that is sent to a number of people. Each letter contains essentially the same text except for a limited amount of information that is specific to each recipient, i.e. their name, address, status, etc.

Using your word processor, you create a standard letter leaving markers in the text where you want to insert the personal data. In addition you generate a data-file containing all the personal data that you want included in the body of the standard letter. When you run a mailing-list program it takes the details for the first person from the data-file and substitutes them into the specified parts of the standard letter. It then repeats this process with the rest of the data-file. The result is a series of standard letters customized for each recipient.

If you were writing a form letter it might look something like this:

10 June, 1985

£Name£
£Company£
£Address1£
£Address2£
£Address3£

Dear £Name£,

I am testing out my new mailing-list package and this letter is designed to show how flexible it is. Please let me know if £Company£ is still the correct name for your business.

Yours sincerely

The text enclosed with £s represents the positions where text will be inserted from the data-file.

A fictitious data-file to accompany this standard letter might be structured like this:

Mr Bark, Doggy Products Ltd., 16 Poodle Lane, Kenneltown, Woofingshire. Mrs Sing, Budgie Toys, 159 Cage Walk, Perchtown, Birdinghamshire. Ms Purr, Cat Food Ltd., 42 Litter Ave., Scratchtown, Pussingshire.

The mailing-list program would produce the following letters:

10 June, 1985

Mr Bark
Doggy Products Ltd.
16 Poodle Lane
Kenneltown
Woofingshire

Dear Mr Bark,

      I am testing out my new mailing-list package and this letter is designed to show how flexible it is. Please let me know if Doggy Products Ltd. is still the correct name for your business.

Yours sincerely

10 June, 1985

Mrs Sing
Budgie Toys
159 Cage Walk
Perchtown
Birdinghamshire

Dear Mrs Sing,

      I am testing out my new mailing-list package and this letter is designed to show how flexible it is. Please let me know if Budgie Toys is still the correct name for your business.

Yours sincerely

10 June, 1985

Ms Purr
Cat Food Ltd.
42 Litter Ave.
Scratchtown
Pussinghshire

Dear Ms Purr,

      I am testing out my new mailing-list package and this letter is designed to show how flexible it is. Please let me know if Cat Food Ltd. is still the correct name for your business.

Yours sincerely

Some packages allow you to produce selective mailing lists from your data-file. For example, you might wish to send a letter to every dog owner in Huddersfield whose name is Scottie or to all the dog owners in London NW10.

    A mailing-list option can be used to print names and addresses directly onto envelopes on continuous stationery or onto sticky labels. Any organization or club that communicates regularly with its membership will find a mailing-list facility invaluable.

Writing aids

It has been estimated that a person of average education has a spoken vocabulary of 10-15,000 words. The proportion of these words that cannot be spelled without consulting a dictionary is difficult to judge but it is probably safe to assume it is a significant number. Even if you do know how to spell your words it is still easy to make typographical errors when typing in your documents. Moreover it is so easy to miss mistakes, particularly your own, when proofreading text. Such an obvious need for some means of automatically checking documents for misspellings has led to spelling aids and dictionaries becoming an integral part of the word-processing scene.

The most elementary kind of spelling-checker enables every word in a document to be checked against an electronic dictionary. Although the size of the dictionary varies from package to package, it is now becoming commonplace to have dictionaries containing 50,000 words on microcomputers.

Most spelling-checkers work in essentially the same way: first they identify the misspelled words and then they provide some means of correcting them in the source document. The program compiles a list of words used in the document and sorts them into alphabetical order. It looks up each word in the dictionary. The words that are found in the dictionary are removed from the list and the remaining words are those suspected of being misspelled.

This brief outline of how spelling-checkers work may mislead you into thinking that selecting a spelling-checker can be reduced to picking the one with the largest dictionary. However identifying misspelled words in a document is by no means a trivial task and spelling-checkers vary considerably in their ability to cope with the problems posed by the English language. Consider this sentence:

the owners of the QL have purchased a state-of-the-art microcomputer which will meet there computing requirements for at least the next tree years.

Let us examine the problems that this sentence poses for a spelling-checker. All the words in the sentence may be found in any reasonable dictionary, yet the sentence contains a number of inaccurately spelled words: a sentence must begin with a capital letter so 'the' should be spelled as 'The'; 'there' has been confused with 'their'; a letter has been omitted from 'three' resulting in 'tree'. A *good* spelling-checker would identify the missing capital letter in 'the'. An *excellent* spelling-checker would be required to identify 'tree' as a misspelling! Also some method has to be found to ensure that the plural form of words is not flagged as a misspelling, e.g. 'owners' and 'requirements'. The dictionary could of course hold the plural and singular forms of each word but this would reduce considerably the number of unique words it contained.

Supplementary dictionaries
Many spelling-checkers originate from the USA and they will happily tell you that 'colour' is incorrectly spelled and suggest you replace it with 'color'. Fortunately the better packages allow you to edit the words in the dictionary so that you can produce an 'English' dictionary instead of an 'American' dictionary. It is also possible to add extra words if necessary. A dictionary tailored to your own needs speeds up the checking process and increases its efficiency.

An option to construct 'supplementary' dictionaries of specialized or technical terms can be very useful. Lawyers could have a supplementary dictionary of legal terms. A technical author might construct a dictionary of scientific words. Supplementary dictionaries are more effiencient than simply adding all the words to one large dictionary. For example, a computer journalist would check all his technical articles against the main dictionary and a supplementary dictionary of computer terms. However a letter to an insurance company would only be checked against the main dictionary.

Commercial dictionaries will not contain the names and addresses of your friends and business contacts. It is usually a good idea to construct a supplementary dictionary of names and addresses, telephone numbers and other personal details that you might refer to in your correspondence, e.g. the name of your dog, the model of your car, etc.

It is now recognized that simply checking words against a dictionary is not sufficient to cope with the complex ways in which errors creep into documents. Spelling-checkers now provide a battery of aids to help you identify mistakes in your text. In fact 'spelling-checker' is no longer an adequate term to describe programs that help with spelling, punctuation, hyphenation and writing style.

Some packages not only identify a misspelled word but also display a list of similar words to help you correct the spelling. Normally the list of likely alternatives is based upon where the mistake occurs in the word. For example, if the mistake was 'foresake', instead of 'forsake', then the list might include 'foresail', 'foresee', 'foreshadow' and so on.

As you can see this might not be very helpful. A sophisticated program would not just list the adjacent words in the dictionary, it would search the rest of the dictionary for other more likely alternatives. One package works on the assumption that words are generally misspelled because the writer:

- adds an extra letter   e.g. 'ressult'
- omits a letter   e.g. 'reult'
- makes a typing error   e.g. 'rasult'
- transposes two letters   e.g. 'reuslt'

Using these 'rules' as the search criteria, a word like 'forewarn' would be found even if it had been entered as 'foreewarn', 'forwarn', 'farewarn' or 'forwearn'.

Another very common writing mistake is to confuse words that have the same sound but completely different meanings. Some common **homonyms**, as these words are called, are 'their' and 'there', 'principle' and 'principal', 'council' and 'counsel' and 'too' and 'to'. A homonym option will mark these commonly confused words in the text, so that you can ensure (insure?) you have used the appropriate word.

Writing aids are now encroaching on the terrain that was previously the preserve of literary editors and human proofreaders. They will identify all sorts of inaccuracies in your documents, such as missing capitals at the beginning of sentences, unclosed quotes and parentheses, incorrect abbreviations and repeated words ('The rain in in Spain'). If you are worried about your writing style then use a program that monitors your text for commonly misused phrases and then offers a number of alternatives. When you are stuck for a word to fit a given context, why not search an on-line thesaurus for some help. Words lose their impact if they are used too often. So keep track of those over-used words with a word-counting program that lists all the words in your document and how often you used them.

Guidelines for improving the readability of documents have been around for years. A typical set of 'rules' might be:

1 Avoid jargon – use the familiar word.
2 Fight sesquipedalianism! If you have a choice use short words.
3 Avoid long rambling sentences.
4 Keep your paragraphs short.
5 Use the active tense not the passive.

A number of programs already exist to compute the readability of text. Several computer magazines have carried articles about formulae for readability which include a listing of a computerized readability program.

These programs produce a number of statistics about your document such as the average number of syllables per word, the average length of the sentences, the average length of the paragraphs, the length of the longest sentence, etc. You should treat all readability formulae with a certain amount of caution. Nobody has ever won the Nobel Prize for Literature by following a readability formula!

Indexing

Organizing a lengthy writing project requires the skills of operational research and the foresight of an astrologer. As each successive draft appears, footnotes become displaced, numbered tables and figures fall out of sequence and cross-references in the text take on the appearance of clues in a treasure hunt. Even when you have completed the final draft you still have the chore of compiling the index, the table of contents and the list of tables and figures.

Document-organizers, or indexing programs as they are normally called, will automatically index all your chapters, sections, sub-sections, figures and tables. In addition they will generate a table of contents and compile an index of all the keywords. A sophisticated package will also keep track of cross-references in the text and maintain a link between the footnotes and their references in the text.

Chapter 11

IMPROVING YOUR DOCUMENTS

By now you should be aware of Quill's extensive range of editing and formatting facilities. It would be a great pity (and a waste!) if you were to use this power simply to increase the productivity of your writing without also trying to improve its quality. Happily in the 500 years since J. Gutenberg started the printing revolution, a number of principles have evolved which can be adopted to increase the effectiveness of your writing.

You might think it is trite to say that good presentation is important. But why is it significant? There are at least two strong reasons why you should pay attention to the layout of your documents. Firstly, information that is badly presented may be difficult to understand or, worse, may lead to actual misunderstandings. Your reader should be able to read your work with the maximum speed and accuracy. This is particularly important if the prospective reader has a *choice* of reading your document or not. Would you plough through a badly organized text if you did not have to? Secondly, poor overall appearance may mislead the reader into assuming that the subject matter is more difficult to understand than it actually is. In this situation some people would be deterred from even attempting to grasp what you are saying.

Visual appearance grows in importance when you consider computer-to-computer communications. It is extremely likely that you will use the QL's powerful communications and networking potential to send messages directly to other computers. In the first instance therefore, the recipient will be viewing your text on a VDU. Most people agree that absorbing information from a screen can be difficult and tiring. In this context it is essential that your message is attractively laid out and easy to read.

Layout

How much flexibility you have in laying out your documents will depend largely on the characteristics of your printer. It is difficult to imagine a worse combination than a cheap dot-matrix printer using fanfold paper. However, if you have a printer with limited facilities do not despair; most of the ideas I am about to discuss will still be relevant to you.

Letter shapes

The letter shapes generated by your printer influence the legibility of your text. We glance at the overall shape of a word and do not decode it letter by letter. Words in capitals have a less varied outline than words in lower case and are generally less easy to understand. It is the ascenders and descenders of lower case letters that produce the distinctive outline required for good legibility. Take a quick look at the program listings reproduced in the popular computing magazines. You will observe that invariably the characters do not have true descenders. This partly explains why they are so difficult to read; y looks like u, q sometimes look like 9, etc.

On a typical typewriter each letter occupies the same amount of space. The problem is that the narrow letters like i and l do not need the same amount of space as, say, the letter M. Equal letter spacing creates an uneven appearance to the text in that some words seem very crowded while others look open. For example, the word illicit is distorted by having too many narrow letters while a word like mummy will seem compressed. Over the years many typefaces have been designed to compensate for this effect. If you are thinking of buying a printer have a close look at how it deals with this problem.

Recognizing the importance of letter shape will help you to decide when it is appropriate to use underlining, capitals or bold text. Underlining should be used with care on cheap printers and poor-quality VDUs. The underline often fuses with the letters above thereby obscuring the letter shapes. In particular avoid underlining words in capitals since these are difficult to read anyway. In fact, research shows that your reading speed is slowed down by as much as 13% when the text is in capitals. So fight the temptation to use large numbers of capitals and restrict them to headings or the occasional word that you want to emphasize. If it is necessary to have a heading followed by a number of sub-headings then put the main heading in capitals and print the sub-headings in bold lower-case with only a leading capital.

HEADING
Sub-heading
Sub-heading

The line   Obviously the more characters you display on a line, the greater amount of text you can see on the screen at any one time. This feature may be useful when creating your text but you should not be deceived into thinking that long line lengths are an asset in your printed document.

Some researchers believe that the optimum line length is between 50-70 characters. With short lines, the normal pattern of eye movements is disturbed too frequently and the eye tends to skip down the page when it returns to the left margin. Long lines cause the eye to return to the beginning of the line just read. Doubling (reading the same line twice) is also influenced by the space between lines. I shall discuss the problem of spacing later in this chapter.

Analysis of line lengths suggests that we might usefully adopt the following method of working. Create your text using the maximum line length available. When it is time to review what you have written adjust the line length to 64 characters. You will now have an ideal line length for both screen editing and your printed document.

If you use a conventional television as a VDU, you have little choice but to use 40-character lines. A television is simply not designed to display text. Make an effort to see some pages on Prestel or Ceefax. You will observe that text is always displayed in short lines with large type. The page designers know the technical limitations of the medium. In contrast, a good monitor will easily display much longer line lengths. Eighty characters per line is the generally accepted standard in the word-processing industry. Incidentally, Wordstar, the world's largest-selling word processor, initially sets its line length to 65 characters.

The use of space   A careful use of space distinguishes good layout from bad and will add to the readability of your documents. I know that worrying about spacing seems a little irrelevant if you are sitting in front of a blank screen or paper unable to write! Think of your documents as fine paintings. You would not put a Van Gogh in a rotten frame. In the same way, treat spacing as the frame for your text.

Margins   It is amazing that so many people take margins for granted. Possibly they are aware that a typical page has four margins – top, bottom, left and right. But I suspect they accept this convention in much the same way they expect to see doors with handles. The function of handles is fairly obvious; the function of margins is less so. Consider the left margin. What size should it be? Pick up a ring binder. Is your document going to be stored in one of these? How wide must the margin be if the holes are not to encroach on the text? Maybe your document is going to be properly bound. In this case text printed close to either edge may curve inwards and be difficult to read. Frequently you will not be able to predict how your document is going to be stored. So be conservative; allow at least an inch for the left and right margin.

You may be fortunate in having a printer with a variety of typefaces. Remember to experiment with the margin settings for each typeface. For example, a small typeface probably requires a fairly narrow margin, otherwise the text gives the impression of being crowded into the middle of the page.

In my view the most aesthetically pleasing layout is to have the left and right margins the same size with the top and bottom margins a littler wider. It is normal to have the bottom margin wider than the top because the eye sees the centre of the page as being slightly above the real centre. If we wish to deceive the eye into believing that our text is centred on the page then we must increase the bottom margin to compensate for the eye's distorted view of the page.

Word spacing and justification

The facility to justify text is often seen as one of the major benefits of using a word processor. Advertisements for word processors are always claiming that justification gives your document a 'professional' appearance. Of course this is true if you are using high-quality typesetting equipment. Unfortunately most of us do not have access to such equipment; instead we are bashing out our documents on cheapish dot-matrix printers. In this context I have to warn you that justified text should carry a Government health warning!

In many years of demonstrating word processors, I have tried to dampen this enthusiasm for justified text. But I have nearly always failed. Although I am pessimistic about my chances, I shall now seek to persuade you to be cautious in your use of justified text.

The problem with justified text is our old friend, the spacing. Quill produces that 'attractive' straight margin by varying the spacing between words. If there is too much space between words then rivers of white space appear to flow down the page. Sometimes this creates the disturbing impression that the text is moving about on the page. Varied spacing is not only visually distracting but it also can act as a form of unintended punctuation. Normally you use commas or full stops to separate the ideas in a sentence or paragraph. The reader is accustomed to the flow of ideas being controlled in this way. However if you are reading and suddenly you come to a wide space between two words you tend to stop and look back to ensure that the words are indeed connnected.

Ragged right margins

The alternative to justified text is the familiar ragged right margin as produced by a typewriter. If you ignore the fashionable preference for justified text and instead concentrate on the needs of your readers then the benefits of unjustified text become more apparent. Equal spacing between words improves readability and largely eliminates the problem of rivers of white space flowing through the documents. Because you do not need to end each line at the right margin, you can allow the content of the text to determine where a particular line should end. For example, you may ensure that a line never ends on the first word of a new sentence or the first word of a subordinate clause. Small points maybe, but they do improve readability of the text and that is surely one of your main priorities.

Hyphens

Unjustified text may look unattractive if there is too much *white space* (the unfilled space) at the end of the lines. Hyphenating words that would extend beyond the margin, rather than carrying them down to the next line, will minimize white space and improve the appearance of a document. The 'rules' for using hyphens are:

● The hyphen must be inserted between syllables.
● Single-letter syllables should not be left dangling at the end of a line (a-round).
● A two-letter syllable must not be carried over to the next line (immediate-ly).

If you find it difficult to identify the syllables in a word, look it up in a dictionary. Any reasonable dictionary not only gives the definitions of words but also the syllables which make up the words. Even if you are addicted to justified text, you will find that sprinkling hyphens throughout your text will greatly improve its readability. Provided you are not too liberal with hyphens – too many will irritate the reader – you can produce documents which are pleasing to the eye and easy to read.

Paragraphing Traditionally the beginning of a paragraph has been indicated by indenting the first line. The white space of the indent helps the eye follow the structure of the text. In my view Quill's default indentation of ten characters is too large, but there is no accepted formula for the width of indents and you will find advocates for indentations of ten or more characters.

Inserting one or more blank lines between paragraphs has become an increasingly popular alternative to indentation as a way of denoting the beginning of paragraphs. Which method you choose is a matter of taste. The important point is not to use both methods and be consistent with your choice.

Tables

Presenting information in tables is often one of the most daunting aspects of writing a report. Tables display a large amount of often complex information in a concise and convenient form. A well organized and carefully laid out table can substitute for pages of prose. On the other hand a poorly presented table with large numbers of columns will deter all but the most committed reader.

Tables vary in complexity but it does not matter whether they contain two or ten columns, they will be used in essentially the same way: an item is selected in one column and then the eye usually scans across the page seeking its relationship with the rest of the data in the row. A careful use of space both between and within the rows and columns will aid the reader in extracting information from the table.

If the table is narrow and has few columns, then there is no need to space out the columns to fill the width of the page. Research seems to show that there is no increase in comprehension if the columns are centred on the page; it is much easier to construct small tables if they start near the left margin. Using wide spacing between columns increases the risk of error as the eye scans across the page.

A wide table containing a large number of columns often benefits from having row headings printed on both sides of the page. The row label on the right-hand side of the page helps to stop the eye wandering down the page as it scans a long row of data.

It is advizable to break up long columns of data with occasional blank lines. A blank line inserted after every fifth item, as you often find in bus timetables, appears to significantly improve information retrieval.

Conclusion

The new generation of word processors like Quill provides an extensive array of formatting commands to improve the appearance of documents. One of the most significant factors in the presentation of information is the use of space. I hope that the guidelines and suggestions made in this chapter will help you to improve the appearance of your documents and in some cases rescue your documents from the ravages that can be inflicted on them by poor-quality printers. Both content and appearance deserve to be treated with respect.

Chapter 12

DATA COMMUNICATIONS

Few people realize that you can gain access to a vast amount of information by connecting your QL to the telephone network. For example, you can display the latest prices on the Hong Kong stock exchange, the timetables for British Rail and, with some banks, the parlous state of your bank account. There are literally hundreds of on-line databases containing such a wide range of information that it is almost equivalent to having the local reference library in your living room.

On-line databases are only a small part of the burgeoning telecommunications industry. If you wish, you can connect your QL to the telex service and send telexes all over the world. If you don't like licking stamps, you might subscribe to British Telecom Gold which is a national electronic mail service. If you are bored with television, there is always Prestel with its mixture of business, travel and entertainment information.

Those people who sneer at 'home' computers – 'What would I use one for? I don't play games' – have completely missed the point. Computers are becoming a key element in business and domestic communications. Look for example at electronic mail: its potential superiority over normal postal services for ordinary letters is probably obvious. However, it is also going to compete with the telephone in many areas. Imagine you wish to contact a friend fairly urgently. You dial the number and there is no reply. You wait ten minutes or maybe half an hour and try again. Once more there is no reply. This routine often goes on for hours. You swear that you will buy them a telephone answering system for Christmas! This whole angst-ridden experience is eliminated with electronic mail. You simply dial up your electronic mail service and leave the message. Your friend arrives home and dials up his 'mail box' and finds the message waiting for him. Even the chore of having to dial up the mail-box service will be unnecessary in the near future. Teletext, the national electronic mail service, will become operational at the end of 1984. With this service, messages will be delivered directly to your QL and either stored on a Microdrive or routed directly to your printer.

If you are sceptical of these claims for electronic mail then consider this new service that has just been announced in the USA. Reachnet is going to be a 24-hour electronic-mail service for lorry drivers. Each lorry will have a small computer and integral printer mounted in the cabin. The drivers can send or receive messages via the system and freight-haulage companies intend to deliver dispatch notes, contracts and all the other paperwork the drivers require, directly into the cabins of their lorries while they are on the road. It is not difficult to envisage how such a system could be used by other companies to keep in contact with their salesmen or their executives while they are away from the office.

The information you gather from on-line databases can be stored as text files on your QL and then incorporated into your Quill documents. Business and financial data may be analysed via your spreadsheet program, Abacus, or incorporated directly into a local database using Archive.

One of the main strengths of the QL is that it has been specifically designed for this new era in computer communications. I shall now discuss the extra equipment and software that you will need to exploit these on-line services.

Modems

A modem (the word is a contraction of the telecommunication terms Modulator-Demodulator) is a device that links your computer to the telephone network. A modem converts the digital signals from the QL into tones that can be transmitted over telephone wires. The telephone system has been designed to carry voice communications, which are completely different to the type of signals generated by the QL. Not only is it a waste of time trying to connect the QL directly to the system, it is also *illegal*. The QL must be connected via a British Telecom approved modem. The output port labelled SER2 on the QL has been designed to work in conjunction with a suitable modem.

Modems may be conveniently divided into two categories: **acoustic couplers** and **directly connected** modems. With an acoustic coupler, you press the telephone handset into a pair of rubber cups. The modem has a tiny speaker which 'speaks' into the mouthpiece and a small microphone that 'listens' to the earpiece. A directly connected modem bypasses the telephone handset and plugs directly into the telephone line through an appropriate jack plug. Sinclair has thoughtfully designed SER2 to accept British Telecom 600-series plugs which are now being used for all new telephone installations.

In general, acoustic couplers are cheap and convenient to use. All you need is a telephone and away you go. However they are vulnerable to stray noise from the environment which may corrupt the signals. Also it is not unusual for telephone handsets to have minor faults which are merely irritating for telephone conversations but are potentially disastrous for computer communications. Incidentally the portability of acoustic couplers is now being undermined by the new fashions in telephone design. Most acoustic couplers are designed to house the traditional handset and they are unable to cope with a world where telephones come in all shapes and sizes. Try attaching one of the 'antique-style' telephones to an acoustic coupler!

Directly connected modems are much less convenient to use because telephone jack sockets are relatively rare in this country in comparison to countries like the USA. Furthermore you may have to disconnect the phone if you wish to use the modem because the connection is often to the jack socket which the phone normally uses. Expensive modems have a voice/data switch so that you can use the phone without disconnecting the modem. The great advantage of directly connected modems over acoustic couplers is that they make a much more reliable connection to the telephone system: the number of data-transmission errors is reduced and they are immune to the effects of environmental noise.

In order for computers to communicate with each other they need to know each others speed of transmission. The speed of transmission is known as the **baud rate**. The definition of baud rate is fairly complex but for most practical purposes you can assume that a speed of 10 baud equals 1 character per second. So if you are communicating at 300 baud you are sending approximately 30 characters per second. The telecommunications industry has standardized on a number of baud rates: 75, 110, 300, 600, 1200, 2400, 4800, 96,000 and 19,200 baud.

Speeds of 75 or 110 baud may seem very slow if you are sending or receiving large amounts of data. Until recently a modem capable of handling speeds up to 300 baud was just about adequate for the domestic user. The advent of services like Prestel, which communicate at 1200 baud, has made these older modems obsolete. I would recommend that you purchase a modem capable of handling speeds up to 1200 baud.

It would be very restricting if you could only send messages. You also need to receive messages even if they are only to confirm that your out-going messages were actually received. Modems are **duplex** devices; they can transmit and receive information. If a modem is capable of sending and receiving information simultaneously, it is said to be operating in **full-duplex** mode. Just as a telephone line allows two people to talk at once on the phone. Some modems are designed for **half-duplex** communications, which means that each party has to take turns in sending and receiving messages. CB radios operate in half-duplex mode; you can either talk or listen but you cannot do both simultaneously. Unlike on a CB radio where you have to flick a switch to change modes, a half-duplex modem is capable of automatically alternating between receiving and sending messages. A modem operating in half-duplex mode takes a finite amount of time to switch between sending and receiving data. This **turnaround** time may be a significant factor if a lot of short messages are being transmitted backwards and forwards along a line. Obviously the lower the baud rate the less important the turnaround time.

In full-duplex mode the characters you type in at the keyboard do not appear on your screen until the 'host' (receiving) computer echoes them back. More precisely, it echoes back what it has received which is not necessarily what you typed in. A minor distortion on a telephone line can so corrupt a message that it would take MI5's largest computer to decipher it! The echoing back of data acts as a check on the accuracy of transmission. Full-duplex mode is generally faster than half-duplex mode and is used for all high-speed communications traffic. High speed is important for a number of reasons:

● It reduces your phone bills; the faster the communications, the less the connect time.
● Your QL is released that much more quickly to do other tasks.
● Accessing remote computers can be a time-consuming process; the faster the speed the less the frustration!

If you use half-duplex to communicate with a 'host' computer, you may see each character you type, duplicated on the screen. This repetition arises because the screen receives one character directly from your keyboard, while the second is echoed back from the host. So, for example, if you typed 'START' in half-duplex mode, the word 'SSTTAARRTT' would appear on the screen. However, the term half-duplex mode does not necessarily signify echoed data. In fact it is often, wrongly, used as a synonym for non-echoed data communications.

Asynchronous and synchronous transmission

I know the heading to this section looks intimidating but resist the temptation to turn the page. The jargon of computing is bad enough, but the terminology of telecommunications is truly horrendous. The complex language, however, disguises the fact that the underlying concepts are fairly simple.

When two computers communicate with each other a number of factors need to be coordinated, in particular:

- the speed of transmission   (baud rate)
- the character codes   (e.g. ASCII)
- the mode of transmission   (asynchronous or synchronous)

For all sorts of technical and efficiency reasons, computers need to be told when a given block of data starts and stops in the continuous stream of information being sent. In **asynchronous** communications, characters are transmitted one at a time and each character is bracketed with a start and stop signal. In **synchronous** communications, groups or blocks of data are sent along the line and each block is prefaced with a start signal and terminated with a stop signal. These stop and start signals are known, not surprisingly, as synchronizing (**synch**) characters.

It is not uncommon to see a bewildering array of acronyms in modem specifications. For example:

- DDCMP   (DEC's Digital Data Communications Message Protocol)
- BISYNC   (an old IBM protocol)
- SDLC   (Synchronous Data-link Control)
- HDLC   (High-level Data-link Control)

These all represent alternative ways to transmitting synchronization information in synchronous communications. Now that you know what they refer to, you can probably forget all about them!

During asychronous communications, the data is transmitted at the same speed as you type it in. The characters do not have to be transmitted at regular intervals because each character carries its own stop and start signal. During synchronous communications, the data is transmitted at a fixed speed with equal spacing between each character. During periods when there is no data to be sent, synch codes are transmitted until further information is ready for transmission.

Synchronous communication is ideal for the high-speed transfer of large volumes of information between computers. Mainframe computers invariably communicate with each other synchronously. The technology required for synchronous communication is much more complex than for asynchronous communications. Consequently modems that can handle synchronous transmissions tend to be the most expensive. Although asynchronous communication is adequate for domestic and small business use, it is gradually being superceded by synchronous communications as modem prices tumble.

**Communica-
tion software**

So far we have concentrated on the 'hardware' aspects of computer communications. To exploit fully all the services available, you will require specialized communications software. In the absence of such software you would be restricted to sending data as you key it in. The option to send files residing on your cartridges would not be available, nor would it be possible to save incoming messages or route them to your printer.

Consider the procedure for accessing Prestel. There you are sitting at home with your Prestel account number, your personal password and your gleaming new modem. You study carefully the instructions for linking to Prestel and you follow them religiously. Instead of the promised 'Welcome to Prestel' appearing on your screen, all you see is pure gibberish. Eventually you discover that you need a special device called a Prestel adaptor to access the service. Your modem takes on the appearance of the proverbial white elephant. The Prestel adaptor solves two problems which our modem is unable to cope with:

● Prestel is based on a non-standard character set which is different to the standard ASCII character set that the QL uses. Prestel has its own unique screen format of 13 lines of 39 characters.
● Prestel expects to receive messages at 75 baud and it replies at 1200 baud (1200/75 sometimes known as 'asymmetric duplex').

Fortunately an alternative exists to buying a Prestel adaptor: a software package that works in conjunction with your existing modem will convert the unique Prestel codes to the QL graphics set and also handle the differing speeds of transmission and reception.

The wide variety of on-line services and their peculiarities (Prestel is by no means unique) makes selecting communications software particularly difficult. In fact no single package will meet all your requirements. To aid you in your choice of software, I have compiled a checklist of the features you should look for in a communications-software package:

● ASCII character set
● Menu-driven
● Meaningful error messages

- Help on-line
- Emulation of dumb terminals
- Full and half-duplex modes
- Selectable baud rates
- File transfer and receipt
- Auto-originate/dial
- Remote access to your files
- Microdrive facilities
- Compliance with CCITT and Bell System standards

I shall now discuss these features and then draw your attention to some of the problems associated with communicating via a PBX or PABX system.

ASCII

Most commercial services recognize ASCII text characters. Consequently you must be careful when transmitting files created with Quill. If you inadvertently use some of Quill's more advanced facilities like bold text and superscripts, the file will contain some control codes that might 'confuse' the host computer. Ideally the communications package should filter out these extraneous codes. Realistically, you may have to restrict yourself to standard ASCII text files for communication purposes.

Menus

The program must be menu driven with the options available at each stage of the program clearly displayed. Well designed menus with self-explanatory prompts will ensure that a program is simple to learn and easy to use. However, once you have mastered the program it should be possible to dispense with the menus and issue the commands directly. The obvious yardstick to use for evaluating a communications package is Quill, which is menu-driven but with a simple command language.

Error messages

If things go wrong (and they will!), it is vital that the software supplies meaningful error messages. Computer programs are notorious for generating obscure and incomprehensible error messages. Look at this example from CP/M, the most well known operating system for microcomputers:

BDOS ERR ON A: BAD SECTOR

This message covers virtually every conceivable problem that might occur with a disk drive, from corrupted disks to broken disk drives. It even appeared if you had simply forgotten to put your disk in the disk drive! An all-encompassing error message like this is next to useless.

Another favourite technique of programmers is to allocate a number to each kind of error. So for example ERROR 21 might appear on the screen and you would be expected to look in the manual or documentation for the explanation of what went wrong. This may not be too much of a chore providing (a) you have the manual to hand and (b) the manual actually clarifies the problem. For, as you will discover, much computer documentation seems to be written on the assumption that you are an experienced programmer. Anyway there is no adequate substitute for meaningful on-screen error messages.

Help
Menu-driven systems by their very nature require the available options to be virtually self-explanatory. This is not always possible and it is extremely useful to have an on-line help facility. If you find that you are unsure about a particular feature of a program, you must have the ability to call up a help file for further information about an option. On Quill, for example, you can hit the F1 key to gain help at any time.

Dumb terminals
The program should enable the QL to simulate a dumb terminal. At present only a minority of customers of on-line databases use microcomputers. The vast majority use computer terminals that are only capable of:

● sending text as it is keyed in
● displaying messages on a screen

Full-duplex and Half-duplex
Ideally both these modes should be available. You will want to use full-duplex mode when communicating with commercial databases and half-duplex mode when you wish to talk to other personal computers.

Selectable baud rate
Occasionally you will want the flexibility to change the baud rate from within the program. The capability to alter the baud rate in this way is especially useful when you are getting a large number of data-transmission errors at a particular speed. Quite often, reducing the baud rate significantly improves the accuracy of data communication.

Sending and receiving ASCII files
The capability to transfer files stored on your Microdrive directly to another computer is one of the main attractions of communications software. The ability to receive files

from another computer and store them on a Microdrive or to route the files directly to a printer is not only useful but absolutely essential if you want to capture files that are larger than your available memory.

Auto-originate/dial
Connecting to databases can be a frustrating, time-consuming procedure of dialling phone numbers, entering account numbers and giving passwords. For example, there is plenty of scope for making mistakes in logging into Prestel. The logon routine involves inputting 21 consecutive numbers: 7 for the phone number, 10 for the account number and 4 more for a password. One error and you will be forced to repeat the whole boring process again. The secret is to get the QL to do it all for you! If your communications package and your modem both support an auto-originate facility then it becomes possible to automate your long procedures. You will be able to longon to Prestel with one simple command. A good package enables you to store all your frequently used logon procedures so that they can be used as and when required. I must emphasize that the auto-originate feature must be supported by the modem as well as the software.

Auto-answer
If you really intend to put your feet up and let the QL take over, then you should let the QL answer the phone as well! Given the appropriate software and a modem with an auto-answer facility, the QL will handle in-coming messages and files without human intervention.

Remote access to your QL
A sophisticated (and expensive) program will enable you to monitor your data communications while you are away from home. Just bear in mind that the capability for remote access to your QL has its dangers as well as advantages. The recent public concern about the security of computer data files should remind you that it is not inconceivable for a malicious person to access your system and wreak havoc with your files. A remote-access facility must be combined with password protection for your files to ensure that there is no anauthorized access.

Microdrive facilities
A good package must be capable of much more than simply saving and transferring files to and from your Microdrives. You will almost certainly want the option to permanently save a complete record of each communications session. Such a file would contain a log of all your in-coming and out-going messages. It is surprising how useful these 'log'

files can be. Large commercial databases can be so complex that learning to use them efficiently is often an expensive process. A chronicle of previous interactions with a database can serve as a reminder of previous successful and unsuccessful search strategies.

A good communications package should be able to handle all the normal 'housekeeping' activities associated with using a Microdrive without disconnecting from the 'host' computer. From within the program, you should be able to check your directory of files, format blank cartridges, delete files to make space for in-coming data, change cartridges, etc. If you begin to run out of space while a file is being received, the program should notify you of the problem and allow you to change cartridges without losing the in-coming data. More expensive packages perform many of the functions normally associated with an operating system.

Telecommunications standards

Most modems in this country operate in accordance with one or more **CCITT** standards. The CCITT is an international organization that sets standards for telecommunications equipment. Modems in the USA comply with a completely different group of standards called Bell System standards. As you might expect these two sets of standards are not necessarily compatible. When you purchase your modem, ensure that it complies with CCITT standards. It is useful if it can operate in accordance with Bell standards as well.

Using a modem in conjunction with a PBX or PABX

Many businesses have their own PBX or PABX telephone system. To make an outside call, you usually dial a single number (usually 9) and then wait for a dialling tone which will signify that you are connected to the national telephone network. You then proceed as if you were on a normal phone. This sequence of operations: wait for internal dialling tone; dial 9; wait for outside dialling tone and then dial number, is simple for a human being but it poses great problems for a modem. You will need expert advice to overcome these problems!

Sending data from your office is difficult; receiving data is virtually impossible. Most private exchanges rely on operators to route calls into the various extensions. This effectively prohibits another computer from contacting your computer directly. The only way to retrieve data from another computer via a PBX or PABX system is for you to originate the communications link (if you can!). Modern PABX systems are now specifically designed to handle computer-to-computer communications.

Conclusion   The combination of QL, modem and communications package is the key to a fascinating world of data communications. If you choose your modem and software with care, you will avoid much of the frustration and expense that is inherent in such a rapidly developing area of technology.

Chapter 13

VISUAL DISPLAY UNITS AND HEALTH

In this chapter my aim is to draw your attention to the controversy over the health hazards of 'new technology'. I can only outline the main areas of concern, as a comprehensive introduction to this subject would merit a complete book in itself. The complexity of the subject makes the use of technical terms unavoidable. I will try to give some explanation of their meaning where it is absolutely essential.

Health and Safety Executive

On 14 June 1983 the Health and Safety Exectutive (HSE) issued a *VDU Guidance Note.* This is generally acknowledged to be the most authoritative document yet to be published on the subject. Its main purpose is to give *advice* to employers on the actions they need to take to fulfil their legal obligations under existing health and safety legislation. Although its publication was welcomed by all sides, some of the conclusions have attracted fierce criticism, particularly from the trades union movement.

When I reviewed the literature on the health hazards of VDUs, I was constantly reminded of this wonderful quotation: 'When two or three economists are gathered together, there are four or five opinions.' Do VDUs constitute a hazard to your health? The literature provides no definite answers. A guarded 'no' is proferred by the HSE; a probable yes is the opinion of the British Society for Social Responsibility in Science (BSSRS). I am afraid there is no alternative to weighing up the evidence and making up your own mind.

I must make it absolutely clear that I am neither a doctor nor an opthalmic optician. Consequently I will not be offering any advice or opinions about this very important aspect of using the QL. In my view too many journalists write as if their doctorates were in medical science and not in computer science. If you were feeling sick, would you pop around to your local computer magazine for a diagnosis? My sole hope is that as a result of reading this chapter, you will have a better understanding of why people are becoming concerned about the indiscriminate use of VDUs.

Possible health risks

The HSE's *VDU Guidance Note* (from now on referred to as the *Note*) discusses the following health hazards:

Radiation
Cataracts
Photosensitive epilepsy
Facial dermatitis
Symptoms and complaints related to postural and visual fatigue
Eye problems

The approach I have adopted is to state the conclusions of the *Note* and then provide a commentary on those conclusions gleaned from my reading of the literature. You should be aware that structuring a discussion in this way may lead to a bias against the conclusion of the HSE since the HSE is not offered the proverbial 'right of reply'. However it does have the great advantage of highlighting the most controversial aspects of the problem. I would urge you not to draw conclusions as to who is right or wrong until you have made your own independent review of the literature.

Radiation
The *Note* states that VDUs probably emit radiation from the whole of the electromagnetic spectrum. In the past most concern had focused on X-ray emissions from the cathode ray tube (CRT) and associated electronic circuits. Attention has now widened to the rest of the spectrum including radio frequency, microwave and ultra-violet radiation.

The *Note* refers to the extensive survey conducted by the National Radiological Protection Board (NRPB) on the radiation emission levels from all types of VDUs manufactured or marketed in the UK.

'The conclusions of the latest survey, in common with those that may be drawn from the many other surveys that have been undertaken, is that national and international limits for continuous exposure are not exceeded. In most regions of the electromagnetic spectrum that were measured, where emissions could be detected, the levels were substantially below existing limits.'

Commentary   We are continually exposed to a variety of radiation emissions from the natural sources, the so-called *background radiation*. The level of background radiation is the standard by which radiation from artificial sources is compared. If a VDU is functioning correctly, it should emit little or no ionization (X-ray) radiation, i.e. the level of emission should be no greater than normal background radiation. All new VDUs seem to comply with this requirement but the worry is that as VDUs get older, the ionization radiation level may increase. Many commentators believe that all VDUs should be tested at regular intervals. This would be comparable with the legal requirement on motor cars to undergo a regular MOT after they have been on the road for three years.

Most surveys have concentrated on the health effects of X-rays; radio-frequency emissions have largely been ignored. The biological effects of this type of radiation are still under investigation. VDUs emit *pulsed*, low-frequency radiation and some commentators contend that low-frequency radiation is more harmful if it is pulsed.

Limits   The *Note* refers to the 'national and international limits for continuous exposure'. A number of critics point out that so little is known of the biological effects of radiation that it is absurd to assume that there are any 'safe limits' for radiation exposure. The continuing controversy over Sellafield (Windscale) is a salutory reminder that the debate about the 'safe limits' of radiation is not restricted to the sphere of new technology. Incidentally, the HSE is currently investigating the problem of ionizing and non-radiation in industry.

Cataracts

The *Note* discusses briefly the supposed link between the use of VDUs and cataracts, a disease which clouds the eye and may lead to blindness if not surgically treated. It notes the suggestion that the cataracts developed by VDU operators 'show a characteristic appearance'. This rather obscure phraseology refers to *capsular cataracts* which are unusual in that the cataract starts at the surface of the lens, unlike most other cataracts which begin in the body of the lens.

The *Note* in effect rejects the contention that using a VDU can cause cataracts. It implies that the balance of the survey evidence is against such a link. Also the 'electromagnetic radiation in the general environment is, by and large,

several orders greater than that obtaining in the vicinity of a
VDU.' The *Note* concludes that 'any hazard, if it exists at all,
must be of a very low order indeed.'

Commentary   The controversy about cataracts received
international publicity in 1977 when two copy editors on
the *New York Times* developed cataracts. Cataracts are
often, though not exclusively, associated with old age. The
copy editors were both young men and they naturally
blamed their condition on the use of VDUs. The US
National Institute of Occupational Safety (NIOS) conducted
an investigation into their claims and concluded that the
radiation levels from their VDUs were not sufficient to
cause their cataracts.

The Newspaper Guild, which represented the two copy
editors, is still not convinced by the conclusions of NIOS.
The union claims that an unusually large number of their
young members have developed cataracts. Dr Milton Zaret,
a doctor who acted as a consultant to the Guild in the
original dispute, has claimed that he has seen a large
number of cataracts caused by radiation levels well below
the supposed safe limit.

The absence of any survey into the long-term effects of
exposure to the low-level radiation emitted by VDUs makes
the trades union movement extremely sceptical of the *Notes*
dismissal of the link between cataracts and VDUs. The
unions believe that the evidence is sufficiently strong to
warrant the introduction of special eye-tests to monitor
cataract development in VDU operators.

Photosensitive epilepsy
The *Note* states, in unambiguous terms, that 'VDU work
does not cause epilepsy and that a person suffering from
this illness should not be prevented from undertaking VDU
work.' The keyword in that sentence is 'cause'. VDUs will
not cause epilepsy to develop in a VDU operator but an
individual who already suffers from a rare form of the
disease, called photosensitive epilepsy, may suffer seizures
through using a VDU. The risk of seizure is related to:

● The size of screen. A large screen increases the risk.
● The refresh rate. The higher the refresh rate the lower
the risk.
● The amount of bright text on the screen. Large
quantities of bright text increase the risk.
● The length of time spent looking at a screen. Prolonged
viewing of a screen at close range increases the risk.
● The angle the screen makes to the eye. Peripheral vision
is particularly sensitive to flicker.

Commentary   Everybody seems to agree that VDUs do not cause epilepsy. Most commentators have concentrated on criticizing the *Note* for not recommending the introduction of equipment that would reduce the risk of seizure. The use of monitors with high refresh rates would significantly reduce the flicker that leads to seizures. In addition a good monitor has a very stable picture that largely eliminates jitter and other types of image instability that might contribute to epileptic seizure. The problem of bright text would be minimized by the introduction of positive-polarity screens which have dark characters on a bright background as opposed to the normal bright characters on a dark background.

Facial dermatitis

Facial skin complaints ranging from 'occasional itching and prickling of the skin to reddening (erythema) and, in a few cases, more substantial rashes' have been reported from around the world. The *Note* attributes most of these problems to environmental factors: low humidity and the static electric field in the vicinity of a VDU. In the event of such complaints, the *Note* recommends that the introduction of humidifiers and anti-static carpeting should be considered.

However some skin complaints appear not to be related to environmental factors. The cause of these complaints remains a mystery but the *Note* specifically rules out radiation as a possible cause. If individuals experience skin complaints which they suspect are related to their VDU work, they are asked to contact the Employment Medical Advisory Service for further advice.

Commentary   Most commentators seem to accept that environmental factors are the most likely cause of facial dermatitis. However it is claimed that the *Note* overlooked one very likely source for these problems: a group of chemicals called polychlorinated biphenyls. These chemicals are used as cooling and insulation agents in the transformers that are often used in VDUs. It is claimed that exposure to these chemicals has been associated with skin rashes.

Symptoms and complaints

The *Note* attributes all other symptoms and complaints to the bodily fatigue associated with using a VDU. It divides symptoms into 'those that are related to the visual system, those relating to working posture and those which reflect the nature and organisation of the work itself.' It suggests that the first two factors can be largely overcome 'by the application of straightforward ergonomic principles in the design, selection and installation of the VDU operator's workplace including the physical environment.'

Commentary Ergonomics comes from the Greek words *ergon* (= work) and *nemein* (= divide) and has been defined as the science of making a job fit the worker. It is an enormous subject and it is not possible to do it justice in a book such as this. There are a number of excellent books and pamphlets on the subject and I urge you to set up your own personal 'workstation' in accordance with sound ergonomic principles.

Pregnancy
The *Note* does **not** mention the controversial reports linking VDUs and miscarriages.

Commentary Many people were disappointed, even dismayed, by the omission of any discussion of the evidence linking VDUs with an abnormally high number of miscarriages amongst VDU operators. As you might expect, an emotive subject such as this leads to a higher than average level of speculation and rumour as to why the *Note* failed to discuss this subject. I won't add to this speculation but I will make the point that the HSE must have been aware of the concern in this area and its omission from the report is, frankly, suspicious.

There have been several reports of clusters of miscarriages occurring amongst VDU operators. However, no comprehensive survey appears to have been completed on this subject. If, and I repeat, if abnormally high numbers of miscarriages are occurring amongst VDU operators, then their cause is not known. Speculation has focused on:

● *Radiation* In particular the controversial low-frequency pulsed radiation.

● *Posture* Many VDU operators in industry and commerce are required to sit for prolonged periods at poorly designed workstations. It is suggested that the resulting unnatural posture adopted by VDU operators may be a contributing factor towards miscarriages.

● *Stress* It is conventional wisdom that intense stress can lead to a miscarriage. The danger from prolonged exposure to low-level stress is less well known. Increases in blood pressure and the level of fatty acids in the blood have all been associated with stressful working environments. Surveys in the USA have demonstrated that VDU operators have a relatively high level of stress.

Obviously the problems of stress and posture are
exacerbated in industry and commerce because the VDU
operators do not have the freedom to take breaks as and
when they feel like it. Stress is a very subjective experience
and some people are much more susceptible to stress than
others.

Eye problems
The *Note* discusses the evidence that eyesight is adversely
affected by VDU work. It states that the 'currently available
evidence suggests that VDU operation is very unlikely to
have a permanent effect upon the eyes or eyesight.'
Furthermore the symptoms of visual fatigue experienced by
some VDU operators is not so extraordinary when you
consider that visual fatigue is associated with many other
industrial and clerical tasks. Consequently the *Note* does
not recommend different visual standards for VDU work as
compared to other clerical work.

It recognizes that wearers of spectacles may need
different prescriptions in order to undertake certain kinds
of VDU work. These individuals are recommended to
consult their optician before commencing VDU work.

Medication   'The use of medication, such as minor
tranquillisers and other psychoactive drugs, is now quite
common. Occasionally side-effects from these substances
may occur which mimic some of the symptoms of visual
fatigue, such as slowing of the eye movements. VDU
operators who may have been prescribed such medication
should be aware of such a possibility.'

Commentary   There is no doubt that the greatest anxiety
about the use of VDUs has been in relation to their possible
effect on the eyesight. Commentators have complained that
the *Note* is making a large assumption when it assures
people that there will be no permanent effects on their
eyesight. In the absence of any detailed survey of the effects
of VDUs on eyesight, it would have been appropriate to
recommend proper procedures to monitor the effect of
VDUs on eyesight. A prerequisite for such a monitoring
exercise would be for each individual to be given an
eyesight test *prior* to commencing VDU work. Any
deterioration in eyesight could then be monitored by a
regular series of eye tests.

The *Note's* very careful wording – 'currently available
evidence suggests' – is an indication that the controversy
about VDUs and eyesight will continue until some proper
research is conducted into the problem.

Your responsibilities   I hope that this brief outline of the VDUs and health debate will stimulate you to conduct your own investigation into the problem. If you are required to use the QL as part of your work, you will need to consider a number of issues that I have been unable to cover in this book: rest pauses, mixing VDU and non-VDU work, positive ions and other environmental factors, etc. New technology is invading all aspects of our lives and it is only sensible to ensure that its undoubted benefits are not marred by avoidable health problems. If you are an employer, you have a responsibility to protect your employees' health, while domestic users of computers have to accept some responsibility for the health of themselves and their families.

Appendix 1

PROTECTING YOUR SOFTWARE AND DATA

Murphy's Law says that 'if something can go wrong it will'.
This law should be etched into the brain of every QL user.
The more dependent you are on your machine, the more
elaborate the precautions you will need to take against
computer malfunctions and loss of data. An analysis of the
most vulnerable parts of your system is the key to
safeguarding your equipment against disaster. You should
conduct the analysis with the same degree of thoroughness
that you would expect of a report from your local
crime-prevention officer. These reports first identify the
main points of entry into your home: windows, doors, drain
pipes, etc., then they outline the appropriate measures to
secure your home against unauthorized entry: burglar
alarms, security locks, etc. You need to compile a similar
report on your computer system.

It is worth beginning with the problems created by three
of the four fundamental elements: air, fire and water.

Air

The air is laden with particles of all shapes and sizes. This
dust is composed of particles of human skin, tobacco
smoke, soot and all the other sorts of pollution produced by
an industrial society. Most large computer installations
have sophisticated air-filtering systems to ward off the
dangers posed by the dust in the atmosphere.

The Microdrives and the cartridges are particularly
susceptible to damage from dust. Dirt sticks to the read/
write heads and eventually leads to excessive wear and tear.
Delicate video tape in the cartridges will be ruined by worn
read/write heads.

Every packet of cigarettes comes with a Government
Health Warning: that smoking can damage your health.

Well it is not only your lungs which are damaged by tobacco deposits, but also your Microdrives. Tobacco smoke penetrates everywhere, coating surfaces with tar and generally gumming up the works. A complete ban on smoking in any room containing computer equipment is increasingly the norm in industry. You will never be able to make your computer room as sterile as an operating theatre, but you can at least bar anyone from smoking near your QL.

Sinclair makes a great point of warning against touching the exposed tape of the cartridges with your greasy fingers. Pay heed to this advice for the oil from your skin will act like a magnet to the dust in the atmosphere. It will lead to a rapid build-up of dirt on the tape which will result in data errors and deterioration of the read/write heads. Never leave cartridges lying about; *always* store them in their boxes when they are not being used.

Fire

Fire is an ever present danger to any house or business premises. A small fire-proof safe is often recommended as an inexpensive method of protecting your files against fire damage. However, if the safe is exposed to very high temperatures, the heat build-up inside the safe may be sufficient to warp the tapes. If you decide to acquire one of these safes, make sure that it has good thermal insulation.

Electronic components are not usually guaranteed to work correctly at very high or very low temperatures. Visitors to large computer installations are invariably surprised at the sharp drop in temperature as they enter the room housing the computer. Temperature is treated so seriously that many computers have automatic shut down procedures if the temperature rises above about 80°F (32°C). As I write it is unclear whether the QL will operate properly at the high temperatures we sometimes experience in summer. Until you know to the contrary, you should assume that the QL may malfunction at temperatures above about 90°F.

Water

The QL never gets thirsty and it doesn't like liquids! Sinclair claim that underneath the keyboard is a membrane which will protect the electronics from an accidental spillage of coffee or tea. Leave it to others to test this claim. Even if the assertion is true, it is likely that the milk and sugar in a drink will clog up the keyboard. Although you could probably clean up the mess without any permanent damage, it is just plain silly to risk ruining your QL for the sake of a cup of tea. Keep drinks away from your QL!

Electricity

Radio-frequency interference

Radio-frequency interference (RFI) or noise may cause problems for your QL. This type of interference may arise from a variety of causes, the most common being the arcing of switches and appliances with electric motors being used on the same ring-main. The QL does have an integral RFI filter and this will cope with all but the worst bouts of RF interference. If you wish to have additional protection for your QL, you can buy, at very little cost, one of the many RFI suppressors on the market.

Power failure

The QL is a very conservative beast when it comes to food: it prefers a nice steady diet of electricity at about 240 volts. Although it is tolerant of small variations in voltage, large fluctuations may lead to a sudden loss of data. Momentary changes in the voltage supplied to your premises may occur at any time. Although complete black-outs are relatively rare thanks to the wonderful National Grid system, there is still the danger to your supply from those anonymous little men in the road clutching those pick-axes. It is only sensible to take into account the possibility of a partial or complete breakdown in your power supply when you are planning your backup procedures.

In practice, switching off your machine accidentally is going to be the most likely cause of a loss of power to your machine! A power failure will lead to an immediate loss of all data and programs stored in RAM and it will almost certainly result in the complete or partial erasure of information stored on your cartridges. Sinclair stress that cartridges must be removed from the QL before it is switched on or off.

Fortunately it is possible to protect the QL from the vagaries of the power supply. There are two options:

1   A device which simply filters out the surges ('glitches') in the voltage supplied.
2   A more sophisticated product that not only suppresses the glitches but also reverts automatically to battery backup in the event of a complete power failure.

There are two kinds of uninterruptible power supply, or UPS as these latter devices are called. A *switched* UPS is normally an 'intelligent' device; it continually monitors the power supply, switching on in a blackout and off when the supply is restored. The change from mains supply to battery backup and *vice versa* has to be accomplished smoothly, otherwise the switch-over may produce a fluctuation in the supply. However a good-quality switched UPS should not cause any problems. A *true* UPS has the battery permanently in series with the mains supply. An interruption to the mains supply does not matter since the power from the battery is sufficient to run the QL. The problems associated with a switched UPS don't apply to a true UPS because the battery is not switched in and out of the power circuit.

Duplicating your software and data

Some people claim that if you chant continually the word OM it brings peace of mind. If you wish to rest assured that your software is safe, then I recommend you chant the word DUPLICATE instead. In my experience there is only one foolproof way of securing your software and data: duplicate everything and then duplicate it all a second time.

I would recommend the following system: make at least three copies of every important software or data cartridge. To a certain extent the measures you take will depend on the kind of commercial software you have. Some packages are specifically designed to prevent you making copies. As a stop to their customers, the suppliers 'generously' offer to supply a replacement copy in the event of corruption – for a fee of course. These products should be avoided. Never purchase any package until you have confirmed that you are allowed to make backup copies for personal use.

As an example, let us look at the measures you should take to protect Quill. Once you have made two copies of the original cartridge, keep two of them with your QL. The third copy is your 'emergency' copy in the event of the two 'working' copies becoming damaged. Ideally the emergency copy should be kept at a friend's or neighbour's house. The philosophy behind this approach is that the emergency copy is isolated from the everyday disasters that might befall the other copies: like, for example, children running riot and putting their greasy little fingers over all your cartridges.

Quill is a commercial package that is relatively easy to replace and you might consider that you don't need such an elaborate security system as outlined above. However, similar reasoning definitely does not apply to your unique data files. It is vital that you adopt the habit of continually duplicating data files. Every time you update a data file you should copy it onto a second cartridge at the end of the session. The third cartridge, housed at a different location, should be updated on a regular basis: once a week, every two weeks, etc., depending on the importance of the data. The third copy is your insurance that you will never lose more than say one week's worth of data.

It is not unusual to keep 'master' copies of cartridges in safety deposit boxes or company safes. The criteria to use when considering your security measures is: 'How much time and/or money will it cost me if I lose these files?'

Copying files and duplicating cartridges is a pretty tedious business and you may be tempted to skimp on your security procedures. If you do you will regret it. I speak from bitter experience!

Earthquakes, floods, volcanoes, hurricanes, etc.

In the UK we are spared most of the natural disasters that regularly afflict much of mankind. The best method of protecting your QL against these disasters is to carry on living in the UK! However we do occasionally get hit by severe electrical storms. Jerry Pournelle, a columnist on *BYTE* magazine, recently mourned the loss of $3000 worth of computer equipment when his house was hit by lightning. The moral of this tale is that Murphy is probably right!

Conclusion

Don't delay. Implement your own disaster-survival plan as soon as possible. Sensible precautions won't cost you an arm and leg and they might well save you a lot of money in the long run. You have been warned!

QUILL COMMANDS

Help	F1	Help
	F2	Prompts
Command	F3	Command menu
menus	F3 O	Second command menu
File-handling	F3 L	Load a file
commands	F3 P	Print a file
	F3 S	Save a file
	F3 Q	Quit
	F3 O F	Files
	F3 O F B	Backup file
	F3 O F F	Format a cartridge
	F3 O F D	Delete a file
	F3 O F I	Import a non-Quill file
	F3 O F ?	List directory of files on Microdrive
	F3 O M	Insert another Quill file at the cursor position
	F3 O Z	Zap
Cursor	CTRL cursor left	Delete character to the left
commands	CTRL cursor right	Delete character to the right
	SHIFT CTRL left	Delete word to the left
	SHIFT CTRL right	Delete word to the right
	CTRL cursor up	Delete all the line to the left of the cursor
	CTRL cursor down	Delete all the line to the right of the cursor

	SHIFT cursor up	Move cursor to paragraph above
	SHIFT cursor down	Move cursor down one paragraph
	F3 G T	GOTO top of file
	F3 G B	GOTO bottom of file
	F3 G \<nnn\>	GOTO top of specified page \<nnn\>

Formatting commands	F3 H	Specify a header
	F3 F	Specify a footer
	F3 O H	Hyphenate
	F3 M	Set margins
	F3 M L	Set left margin
	F3 M R	Set right margin
	F3 M I	Set indent margin
	F3 J	Justify
	F3 J L	Left justification
	F3 J R	Right justification
	F3 J C	Centred justification
	F3 T	Set tabs
	F3 P	Unconditional page break
	F3 D	Design
	FD O V	View a wide document
	F4	Typeface
	F4 B	Bold text
	F4 U	Underline text
	F4 H	Superscript
	F4 L	Subscript

| Block commands | F3 C | Copy or move block of text |
| | F3 E | Erase block of text |

| Search and replace commands | F3 O S | Search for specified text |
| | F3 O R | Search and replace |

| Miscellaneous command | SHIFT F4 | Insert/overwrite mode |

Command	Cursor left	Move one character to the left
line editor	Cursor right	Move one character to the right
	Cursor up	Move to beginning of command line
	Cursor down	Move to end of command line
	CTRL cursor left	Delete character to the left
	CTRL cursor right	Delete character to the right
	CTRL cursor up	Delete all characters on line to the left
	CTRL cursor down	Delete all characters on line to the right
	SHIFT cursor left	Move left by one word
	SHIFT cursor right	Move right by one word

GLOSSARY

A4   Standard size for office paper in UK. It measures 297 mm by 210 mm.

ABORT   To deliberately stop an action such as a command in one of the programs supplied with the QL, or the execution of a program.

ACK   A control code used to denote that a message has been accepted.

Alphanumeric   Strictly the letters A to Z, a to z and the numbers 0 to 9. Frequently extended to cover the punctuation symbols.

Applications package   Computer programs which perform a specific task such as word processing, accounts payable, bill of materials, etc.

ASCII   American Standard Code for Information Interchange. An internationally accepted way of representing characters in binary code.

Asynchronous communications   A method of transmitting information. Transmission is synchronized by the addition of a start and stop bit to each 'byte' or character sent. The time intervals between each character may be of unequal length.

Auto-boot   A feature of an operating system that allows a program to be automatically loaded and run without the user having to give an explicit load and run command.

Backup   A commonly used piece of jargon denoting any procedure that provides protection against computer malfunction, software failure, or data corruption. Used as in 'making backup copies of my files'.

Bandwidth   The range of frequencies available for transmission of information in a communications system. The width is expressed in Hertz (Hz) and is a measure of the amount of information that may be sent in a given time.

Baud   The rate of data transmission, measured in bits per second. Because of the presence of stop and start bits, not directly convertible to characters per second. Rule of thumb: 10 baud = 1 character/second.

Bi-directional   In connection with printers, it is the ability of a printer to print in both directions: from left to right and from right to left. An alternative term is *boustrophedon* which means 'like an ox ploughing'. Rarely used because nobody is able to spell it, never mind pronounce it!

Bit   The abbreviation of binary digit. A bit has a value of either '0' or '1'. Bits are usually grouped in bytes (8 bits). It is the smallest unit of information used by a computer.

Buffer   A device or section of memory where data is temporarily stored when information is being transferred between devices. The components of a computer system work at radically different speeds. A buffer compensates for the difference in speed of data handling when devices communicate with each other.

Bugs   Mainly used to denote errors in computer programs. The process of correcting mistakes in programs is known as 'debugging'.

Byte   Generally accepted as a set of 8 bits. A byte is used to represent one character, e.g. in ASCII.

Carriage return   A control code which causes the print-head on a printer or the cursor on a screen to move to the left margin. Often used in conjunction with a linefeed. The ENTER key on the QL generates a carriage return and a line-feed.

Cathode ray tube   Abbreviated to CRT. A device used to generate pictures as in a television or monitor.

CCITT   Consultative Committee on International Telephone and Telegraphy. A treaty organisation which sets standards for communications equipment and systems.

Centronics   A very popular parallel interface for connecting printers to computers. *See* Parallel.

Character set   The total number of different characters of the same style or font available on a computer or printer.

Control codes   Probably best explained by examples. ACK and ETX are control codes. Some computer terminals use 'escape sequences' to manipulate the screen, e.g. ESCAPE J might clear the screen, ESCAPE H sends the cursor to top of screen.

CPU   Central Processing Unit. No accepted definition. Essentially it is the 'brains' of the QL: the chips which carry out the logical and arithmetic processes.

Cursor   The little square on your screen showing where the next character you type will be displayed.

Daisywheel   A flat disk with spokes radiating from a hub. At the end of each spoke is a character. It resembles a daisy, hence the name. Printers that use daisywheels are called daisywheel printers.

Data   The information which is processed, stored and transmitted by a computer. Someone (I forget who) once wrote that data is to computers what information is to human beings.

Database   (As in on-line database.) A large file or collection of files designed to be shared by several users.

Debug   *See* BUG.

Dedicated   A machine used specifically for one kind of work. Some machines only do word processing; these are called 'dedicated' word processors to differentiate them from machines like the QL which can do a lot of other things as well as word processing.

Descender   The portion of a lower case letter (and sometimes the downward stroke of a 'Q' that descends below the line. The letters g, j, p, q, and y have descenders.

Diablo   Often used as a synonym for daisywheel printers. It is derived from the name of one of the world's largest printer manufacturers.

Directory   (As in directory of files on a cartridge or disk.) The list of files on a cartridge; contains the name, size and location of each file on the cartridge.

Dot-matrix   A method of printing using an array of dots to represent a character.

Dumb terminal   A device which can only transmit or receive data to and from a computer. *Contrast with* Intelligent terminal.

Duplex   A method of communication that allows transmission in both directions.

Duplex (full)   A method of communication that allows *simultaneous* transmission in both directions.

Duplex (half)   A method of communication that allows transmission in both directions but *not* at the same time.

Ergonomics   Refers to the planning and design of working environments. An ergonomic design takes special care to incorporate the needs of human beings.

Error message   A message from a device which signifies that an error has been encountered in the hardware or software.

Error rate   Ratio of the number of bits or characters *incorrectly* received to the number of bits and characters transmitted.

ETX   A control code used to signify the end of transmission. Used in conjunction with ACK.

Fanfold   Computer paper which is folded like a

concertina. Each fold is in the opposite direction to the previous one.

Field   Data records are composed of fields. A record containing names and addresses might have the name in the first field, the number and road name in the second field, the town in the third field, etc.

File   A collection of data records. It might contain data or programs, or both together.

Firmware   A program permanently stored in a memory chip (ROM).

Floppy disk   A thin, flexible, magnetic disk enclosed in a protective cardboard jacket. Used to store programs and data. There are two main sizes: 5¼ inch and 8 inch.

Font (or fount)   A set of characters in a particular style of type.

Friction-feed   Refers to a method of advancing paper through a printer using the friction between the paper and the roller (platen).

Fully formed characters   Complete characters as you would find on a typewriter. Fully formed characters produce the best possible print quality. *Contrast with* Dot-matrix.

Function keys   Special keys that may be used in application programs to denote frequently used commands.

Glitch   A burst of electrical noise that is strong enough to affect your QL.

Hard copy   What you see on the screen is soft copy. What the printer produces is hard copy.

Hard disk   A rigid disk enclosed in an air-tight container. It is capable of storing large amounts of data. A hard disk capable of holding 5 million characters is promised for the QL (5 Mbyte). (Hard disks are often known as Winchesters.)

Hardware   The physical components that make up a computer system: ROM, RAM, disks, printer, VDU, etc.

IBM   Incredibly **B**ig **M**ultinational company! Seriously, the world's largest computer company.

Intelligent terminal   A computer terminal that is able to do a limited amount of data processing independently of its host computer.

Interface   A device or electronic circuit that allows two different machines to communicate with each other, e.g. the RS232C and Centronics interfaces.

I/O   Input-output. The communication of information to and from a computer or peripheral device.

I/O port   *See* Port.

Justify   In word processing, the forming of a straight right-hand margin by the elimination of leading or by trailing spaces.

K   Symbol for 1024 bytes.

Kb or kb   Alternative symbol for 1024 bytes, known as 1 kilobyte or 1 kbyte.

Letter-quality   Generally associated with the output produced by daisywheel or laser printers.

Line-feed   A control code that causes the printhead on a printer or the cursor on a screen to advance by one line.

Line spacing   The number of lines per inch.

Logic-seeking   The ability of a printer to move the printhead by the shortest or most efficient route to the next printing position.

M   Symbol for 1 million bytes, or 1 Mbyte.

Matrix   *See* Dot-matrix.

Mainframe   A term commonly used to describe large computers.

Mb   Alternative symbol for 1 million bytes.

Memory   General term describing the data storage facilities on a computer. In microcomputers, there are two main types of memory, ROM and RAM. The amount of memory is normally quoted as so many K.

Menus   A list of options, one of which can be selected at any time.

Multitasking   The ability to execute two or more programs simultaneously. The QL has a multitasking operating system.

Near-letter-quality   NLP. The best output that presently can be produced by dot-matrix printers. Still falls short of the quality produced by printers using fully formed characters.

Network   (As in computer network.) A system that enables computers to communicate with each other and allows them to share expensive peripherals like printers and hard disks.

Operating system   The program in a computer that controls all the standard operations of the computer: reading and writing from and to the Microdrives, allocating memory to programs, supervising input/ output, etc.

Output   The end-product; the result of running a program; the printout of a document created with, for example, QL QUILL.

PABX   Private Automatic Branch Exchange. An in-house telephone system that can function without telephone operators.

Package   (As in software package.) Jargon for programs like QUILL, EASEL, etc.

Parallel   A mode of transmission in which all the bits in a byte are sent simultaneously. *Contrast with* Serial.

PBX   Private Branch Exchange. An in-house telephone system that requires telephone operators to handle incoming and outgoing calls.

Peripherals   (As in peripheral equipment.) Refers to the other devices that are attached to computers: disks, printers, modems, etc.

Pitch   The number of characters per inch.

Pixels   Sometimes known as a picture element. The 'points' or 'dots' that make up an image on a screen.

Points   Type size measured in units of approximately 0.014 inch, i.e. approximately 72 to the inch.

Port   A socket on a computer into which you can connect a printer or modem, or indeed any other peripheral device.

Print wheel   *See* Daisywheel.

Program   A series of instructions to be executed by a computer.

Proportional spacing   Refers to the spacing of individual characters. In proportional spacing, narrow letters like 'I' are allocated less space than wider letters like 'm'.

Protocol   A set of rules or conventions governing the transfer of information, e.g. ETX/ACK.

QL   *As in* if the QL lives up to its specification it will make every other business computer on the market look very over-priced.

Quit   To stop a program from executing. When you decide to stop using a program, you are said to quit the program.

QWERTY   The traditional layout of keys on a typewriter. The term is derived from the sequence of letters on the uppermost row of alphabetic keys.

RAM   Random Access Memory. Sometimes known as read/write memory. This is where the QL stores your programs and data. It is volatile, i.e. when you switch off the power all the data stored in RAM is lost.

Reset   (As in reset the QL.) Returns the machine to the state it would be in if you had just switched on. All programs and data stored in RAM are lost when you do a reset.

ROM   Read Only Memory. As its name implies, you can only read the data stored in ROM. SuperBASIC is stored in a ROM in the QL. It is non-volatile in that switching off the power has no effect on the data stored in ROM.

RS232C   A serial interface that has almost become the internationally accepted standard.

Run   First you load a program into memory and then you execute the program. Run is the command to tell the QL to execute the instructions in a program.

Serial   A mode of transmission in which the bits in a byte are sent sequentially along the line. *Contrast with* Parallel.

Software   *See* Program.

String   Jargon for a group of characters. This sentence is a 'string' of characters. Has a more specialised meaning in the context of BASIC programming.

Terminal   *See* Dumb terminal.

Tractor-feed   A mechanism for feeding fanfold paper through a printer. The holes in the paper fit into two gear-like wheels which drag the paper through the printer as they rotate.

Typewriter   An obsolete machine that you used before you had QL QUILL.

Update   To modify a file with new or additional data.

User-friendly   (As in user-friendly program.) A description of software that has been written on the assumption that (a) you don't have a degree in computer science and (b) you are not telephathic and you can't read the programmer's mind.

VDU   Visual Display Unit. Sometimes known as a Visual Display Terminal (VDT). Essentially a monitor or television. Definition may extend to terminals with an integral keyboard.

Winchester   *See* Hard disk.

Word processing   Use QL QUILL.

XOFF   A control code used to tell a computer to stop transmitting.

XON   A control code used to tell a computer to start transmitting.

INDEX

For ease of identification, commands appear in single quotes